# Language  *An Introduction*

*Louis Hjelmslev*

# Language  *An Introduction*

*Sproget*, translated

from the Danish

by Francis J. Whitfield

*The University of*

*Wisconsin Press*

*Madison, Milwaukee*

*and London 1970*

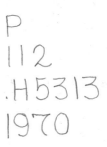

Published by the University of Wisconsin Press, Box 1379, Madison, Wisconsin 53701

The University of Wisconsin Press, Ltd., 27–29 Whitfield Street, London, W.1

*Sproget: En introduktion* originally published by Berlingske Forlag, Copenhagen, 1963

Printed in the United States of America by George Banta Company, Inc., Menasha, Wisconsin

SBN 299–05640–6

LC 70–98119

# Contents

# Translator's
# Introduction

Although the Danish original of this book (entitled *Sproget: En introduktion*) was not published until December 3, 1963, it was actually composed some twenty years earlier. It thus belongs to that extraordinarily creative period in Hjelmslev's life—resplendent with his vision of a new, *"linguistic* linguistics"—that also produced the *Prolegomena to a Theory of Language (Omkring sprogteoriens grundlæggelse)* and, among works now awaiting posthumous publication, the *Résumé of a Theory of Language (Sprogteori: Résumé)*. In contrast to the *Résumé*'s compendious, formal exposition of the "glossematic" theory, both the *Prolegomena* and *Language* were conceived as popularizations: the former as an outline, addressed to a scholarly audience, of the foundations of glossematics; the latter (in which the word *glossematics* does not once appear) as an introduction, primarily for laymen, into the problems of language and its scientific study.

An immediately striking contrast between the two "popular" works is to be accounted for by this difference of intended audience. A large portion of *Language* is concerned with the subject of genetic relationship between languages, and the structure of the whole book is determined by the central importance attached to the different possible relationships, genetic and nongenetic, that languages may have with one another. In the *Prolegomena*, on the other hand, attention is mainly directed to relationships within the individual language and within its texts. If, however, the reader is tempted to view the two books as in some way dividing the fields of comparative and descriptive linguistics between them, he courts serious danger of misreading them both. For one thing, the several discussions of internal relationships that he will find in the present work must be seen as necessary, organic parts of its argument. For another, it would be a superficial reading (however common) of the *Prolegomena* that ignored the final chapter and its express warning that "it is not the individual language alone that is the object of the linguist."

To Hjelmslev it was obvious that linguistics must be "comparative," not for mere comparison's sake, but for the successful pursuit of its true aims. The conclusion of the *Prolegomena* makes this quite apparent, even though the body of that work is devoted—as it could be devoted, in view of its special audience— to other aspects of the linguistic science that the author envisioned. It was equally obvious to Hjelmslev that an appropriate introduction to the study of language, both for the layman and for the linguist who wishes to review the bases of his discipline, must be through the portal of comparative grammar —in particular, the comparative grammar of Indo-European. In his review[1] of Louis H. Gray's *Foundations of Language* he had written unequivocally:

> Un mérite qui sera accueilli sans doute avec une satisfaction particulière est qu'il est tenu compte dans une très large mesure des faits et des théories indo-européens. L'indo-européen reste le stock où le linguiste de tous temps puisera de préférence ses matériaux et ses exemples; en outre l'indo-européen est le seul domaine linguistique que nous *croyions* [italics added—FJW] vraiment connaître à fond. Il est donc oiseux de vouloir éviter au lecteur les difficultés techniques de la grammaire comparée; ce serait le tromper et lui dérober l'essentiel; il faut au contraire saisir le taureau par les cornes et faire ce que M. Gray a fait: introduire dans les problèmes de la linguistique générale en les regardant à travers les faits indo-européens. Ce procédé seul permettra de faire comprendre au lecteur que malgré tout la linguistique est une science, sinon dans la théorie, du moins dans la technique, et de le laisser pénétrer, à titre d'observateur, dans le laboratoire du savant. Rien de plus dangereux que de dissimuler au spectateur les difficultés réelles, et de lui faire croire qu'on peut étudier avec profit la linguistique générale sans des connaissances de grammaire comparée. Les conséquences de ces mirages ne laissent

1. *Acta Linguistica* 2.1 (1940–41): 122–26.

pas de se faire sentir dans le monde scientifique même, et contribuent largement à aggraver le schisme entre deux disciplines qui ont constamment besoin l'une de l'autre, et à répandre le dilettantisme dans la linguistique théorique. Linguistique générale sans grammaire comparée est une linguistique en l'air.

The review of Gray must be read in its entirety by anyone who would learn more of Hjelmslev's preparation for the task he was to undertake in writing *Language*. At the very beginning of the review, he enumerates, without any claim to having made a complete list, twenty-six general works on language that had appeared in the nineteenth century, and thirty-one in the first four decades of the twentieth, and he acknowledges the need to which this accelerating production is a response. But the difficulties of meeting that need are enormous:

> Les fondements de la linguistique sont controversés, aujourd'hui plus que jamais. Les exploits théoriques n'égalent pas le besoin pratique d'un traité d'ensemble embrassant toutes les branches de notre science d'un point de vue unique et communément adopté. La linguistique peut devenir une science; elle ne l'est pas encore; les qualités essentielles d'une science, l'objectivité et la précision, lui manquent encore dans une très large mesure. Les exposés dont on vient de parler en portent souvent fatalement l'empreinte; beaucoup d'entre eux souffrent de subjectivité et d'exclusivité; souvent ils ont été écrits pour propager des vues particulières, bien que souvent originales; il en est qui sont des guides franchement infidèles. . . . D'entre les nombreux exposés qui existent il n'y a donc guère un seul qui puisse servir comme véritable manuel au non-initié ou au débutant, ni comme guide principal au lecteur averti.

Even Gray, despite the incontestable merits of his book, is found to have been led by his impartial attitude into a certain eclecticism "qui ne peut pas toujours réussir," and the reviewer concludes:

> Publier un livre sur la linguistique est un travail vraiment ingrat, et c'est la linguistique et non l'auteur qui est en faute. A moins de vouloir viser le but suprême qui consiste à présenter une doctrine purement personnelle et en même temps solide (et à notre avis il

n'y a que F. de Saussure qui y ait réussi complètement) on est réduit
à présenter un compromis où tout ne peut pas être au même niveau.

There can be no doubt that when Hjelmslev himself decided
to undertake the "thankless task," even though within the
miniature frames of what he called a popular survey, it was the
"supreme goal" that he aimed at and it was the model of Saussure
that he kept in view. *Language* is a confessedly personal book
that nevertheless boldly asserts its claim to being a solid one,
free of the subjectivity for which Hjelmslev had reproached
others.

The reader may find a paradox here, if not a contradiction,
but Hjelmslev sets forth the claim with confidence, relying,
above all, on his care in distinguishing between "what we know
with certainty and what we do not know with certainty" (*hvad
vi med sikkerhed véd og hvad vi ikke med sikkerhed véd*). This
phrase, interestingly enough, finds its echo in the centennial
lecture that Hjelmslev delivered in honor of his eminent pre-
decessor Vilhelm Thomsen,[2] where we read: "He wished to distinguish, and distinguished everywhere as sharply as possible,
between, as he says, 'what can be known' and 'what must remain only rough hypothesis': between what one knows with certainty and what one does not know with certainty." The same
lecture also gives strong indication of another respect in which
Thomsen served as an exemplar, and that is in the matter of
style. In discussing Thomsen's *History of Linguistic Science*,
Hjelmslev observes: "The style is unpretentious, plain, and
simple, but by its very artlessness stands forth with an extraordinary dignity and a quiet distinction. The elegance lies in
the content alone, never in the form; the form is the simplest
possible, and its merit lies precisely in the fact that it does not
assert itself, but imperceptibly, faultlessly, smoothly, provides
just what is needed for the content to act on the listener with all
its carefully calculated weight. A mild and friendly tone per-

2. "Vilhelm Thomsen. Foredrag paa Københavns universitet 26. januar
1942," *Gads danske Magasin* (1942), pp. 136–47.

vades the exposition, a subdued humor lies ready to give color where occasion naturally arises." A better characterization of Hjelmslev's own style in *Sproget* I could not imagine.

Even the briefest discussion of the background of this book would be incomplete without special mention of one more linguist: Edward Sapir. In Hjelmslev's necrology of Sapir,[3] it is again the scholar's respect for facts—together with the use that he makes of them—that is emphasized:

> Sapir was constantly on his guard against hasty generalizations and sentimental prejudices; but this attitude did not involve sterile inductivism; Sapir was a highly visionary and synthetic mind, but his general theories were constantly checked by his knowledge of facts. Sapir's method was empiricism in the best sense of the word: his doctrine was theory built on experience. The reader of Sapir's works has the constant feeling that facts are not stated in order to provide him with knowledge for its own sake, but only to provide him with the material necessary for thinking. . . . Sapir's theory of language inspires with confidence because the only confidence he has in it himself is in the facts. For this reason Sapir's *Language* (1921) is likely to hold its place as a classical work and as one of the very best introductions to general linguistics yet written. The present writer clearly remembers the time when he first read it; it was a revelation, a confirmation of his vague anticipation of the possibility of establishing a *comparative general linguistics* destined to supersede the subjective and sentimental *philosophy of language* of the past.

Not surprisingly, Sapir's *Language* heads the list of suggested reading appended to Hjelmslev's own book. Although, out of considerations of appropriateness, I have elected not to reproduce this list in the English edition, it is interesting to examine the titles that it includes of works published before 1944. Among the recommended general introductions, Sapir's is followed by Vendryes' *Le langage*, Sandfeld's *Sprogvidenskaben*, Marouzeau's *La linguistique*, Jespersen's *Philosophy of Grammar*, Pedersen's *Sprogvidenskaben i det nittende århundrede*, Graff's *Language and Languages*, Bloomfield's *Language*, Gray's *Foundations of Language*, Skautrup's "Sproget" (in *Alverdens Viden*

3. *Acta Linguistica* 1.1 (1939): 76–77.

*III*) and Collinder's *Introduktion i språkvetenskapen*. Saussure's *Cours de linguistique générale* appears, curiously enough, not among the general works, but in the references under "Linguistic Change," where special mention is also made of his "Mémoire sur le système primitif des voyelles dans les langues indo-européennes." The only reference under "Sign Formation" is to Grammont's *Traité de phonétique*, and the only one under "Linguistic Structure and Linguistic Usage" is to Gardiner's *Theory of Speech and Language*, described as "a presentation of the same problem from a somewhat different point of view." Hjelmslev's own *Omkring sprogteoriens grundlæggelse* appears as suggested further reading on "Types of Linguistic Structure," while Jespersen's *Modersmålets fonetik* and Jakobson's *Kindersprache, Aphasie und allgemeine Lautgesetze* find their place under "Types of Linguistic Usage." "Genetic Relationship" is represented by Meillet's *Introduction à l'étude comparative des langues indo-européennes*, Schrijnen's *Einführung in das Studium der indogermanischen Sprachwissenschaft*, and Charpentier's *Jämförande indoeuropeisk språkvetenskap*. References under "Language Families" are to Lombard's *Europas och den vita rasens språk*, to Kieckers' *Die Sprachstämme der Erde*, and to *Les Langues du Monde*. Schrader's *Sprachvergleichung und Urgeschichte* and Vilhelm Thomsen's "Oldarisk kultur" (in the first volume of his *Samlede afhandlinger*) are the recommended readings on "Parent Languages."

A few words remain to be added about the present version of the book. Besides the reading list just mentioned, I have eliminated another appendix that was more appropriate to the original edition than it would have been to this one—a short collection of selected terms and their definitions, together with some very brief biographical notes on linguists mentioned in the text. As translator, I have not thought it any part of my duty to conceal the fact that the book was originally addressed to a Danish audience: thus, the reader will find Latium still compared in size to Zealand (2700 square miles), and counter-examples introduced by an analogy with the legal situation on the Faeroes. At the same time, I have freely replaced or modified illustrative examples which, because of the knowledge of Danish that they presupposed or for other reasons, would have required the addition of distracting footnotes. In matters of terminology, I have deviated from the original in a few instances. I have used "relation" and "correlation" in the technical senses given to those words in the *Prolegomena*, simply because I found no other way of rendering, without risk of confusion, the less formal terms that Hjelmslev used in *Sproget*. I should also note particularly that the English text has expression elements "represented" by sounds or letters, where the Danish uses words that would normally be translated "named" or "signified." I can believe that Hjelmslev might, in English, have preferred "symbolized," but, with some misgivings, I have settled on a relatively neutral substitute.

The final chapter, on languages of different degrees, is not included in the Danish edition. It did, however, originally constitute the conclusion of the book, as I discovered in 1967 when reviewing Hjelmslev's papers at the gracious invitation of Mrs Hjelmslev. Although passing years have obscured the history of this lost chapter, it would appear that Hjelmslev had at some time been persuaded that it was too difficult for a popular audience and that the book could be reduced to a more reasonable length by its omission. However that may be, it was preserved in fair copy, and it clearly represents the summation of all that has gone before. For these reasons I have not hesitated to include it here. The attentive reader may find it particularly helpful in dispelling the curious misconceptions that have arisen about Hjelmslev's supposed "neglect of substance" and exclusive preoccupation with form.

Louis Hjelmslev authorized me to undertake the translation. I offer it to Vibeke Hjelmslev with my warmest gratitude.

F. J. W.

*Berkeley*
*October 3, 1969*

# Language   *An Introduction*

# Prefatory Remarks

The science of language, or linguistics (from Latin *lingua* 'a language'), has—like every other science—had its classical and its critical periods. In the classical periods there has been an established body, or structure, of doctrine, agreed on and respected by everyone, and scientific work has been concerned with details that could be fitted into the frames of that structure. In the critical periods, investigators have been occupied with the structure itself, which they have tried to establish on new and better foundations, reflecting a deeper and more penetrating appreciation of the nature of language.

Never, perhaps, has linguistics passed through a critical period of such profundity and scope as in our time. The very nature of language and its structural peculiarities are now being debated by linguists. The very basis of linguistics is being recast. This is not, of course, to be understood as meaning that linguists have ceased to be concerned with details. But even in their work on details they are constantly being faced with problems of foundations, to a much higher degree than ever before. This concern with foundations has already taken us so far from earlier notions that the new linguistics of our time can be contrasted to all former varieties, which can be grouped together under the common name of *classical linguistics*. Sooner or later the present crisis must necessarily lead to a new classicism. Perhaps we may even now say that we have come far enough to make out at least the contours of such a new classicism, but we have not yet attained it, and there is no agreement about the ways and means of doing so.

Such a crisis is not to be deplored—quite the contrary. The

critical periods are the refreshing and inspiring ones, proving that science is not stagnant but is constantly renewing itself. And the critical periods broaden our horizon and deepen our understanding of the things that have the most importance of all. Indeed, so great has been this effect of the present crisis that we may venture to assert that only now has linguistics succeeded in organizing itself as an independent science.

It is possible to be interested in language from many different points of view. The ancient Greeks and Romans and the medi-æval scholastics were interested in it mainly from the logical point of view; and it was in close association with Aristotelian logic that they founded a grammatical tradition still surviving in our school grammar and, with little change, even in most of our scientific grammar in its classical forms. In the eighteenth and nineteenth centuries, many scholars came to be interested in language principally from an historical and prehistorical point of view, with particular reference to cultural history, so that the history and relationships of languages were seen as a reflexion of, and as a means of knowing, the history and relationships of peoples. In the nineteenth century arose the special science that called itself phonology or phonetics, interested in language from a physiological and physical point of view and attempting to describe the expression plane of language through a study of the movements and positions of the speech organs in the production of speech sounds and through a study of the sound waves that are so produced. There also arose in the nineteenth century a linguistic psychology, which saw in the psychological side of language, in language as a part of man's "mental life," the essential feature in the nature of language. And down to our own time, sociological considerations in ever-increasing measure have been brought to bear on language considered as a social institution.

Evidently, there is no lack of points of view from which language can be, and has been, studied. But none of these (and more could easily be added) provides the basis for an independent science of language; rather, language becomes an object of study, now for logic, now for history, now for physiology, physics, psychology, or sociology. And it can be argued that despite all this many-sided study, one point of view about language has been neglected and, at that, the one that seems the most important and the most natural—the *linguistic* point of view. It should be possible to imagine a science that does not take language simply as a conglomerate of logical, historical, physiological, physical, psychological, and sociological factors, but first and foremost as an independent entity, an integral formation of a special kind. Only such an integral view can account for the fact that all these apparently so heterogeneous elements are able to come together in language. The linguistic point of view, taken as the central one, can determine the relative justification and the relative limitation of each of the particular points of view. Only when the logical, historical, physiological, physical, psychological, and sociological linguistics are complemented by a *linguistic* linguistics can an autonomous science of language be established. It is in a struggle to this end that our present crisis finds us.

Any exposition made today of the problem of language must necessarily reflect this situation—both for good and for ill. One advantage deriving from this critical debate is that we believe we have reached a clear understanding of many things that formerly either went simply unnoticed or were viewed in a quite different light. One disadvantage is the multiplicity of discordant voices echoing round the author as he writes. It would hardly be possible, in a popular survey like this, to allow all these many voices to be heard and to introduce them directly into the critical debate. And it would serve little purpose, as well. There are many—indeed, many important—points at which one dares to break into the debate, strike out, and say: this is the way things are, and that is not the way things are. And it would be time-wasting and confusing to explain that there are people who have thought, or who perhaps still think, that things are different.

Many positions have been held without any justification in the earlier, subjective period of linguistics. Through the present crisis, justification, argumentation, and proof are demanded, and opinions offered without justification need be neither reported nor refuted: they will die of their own accord.

The reader must realize, however, that it is hardly possible to set up a complete system at the present time. In many respects, the exposition that follows must aim at posing problems rather than solving them. This book, then, is designed as an introduction to the *problem* of language as, *in the author's judgment*, it stands today.

The reader should also understand two things:

1. Our presentation is *not subjective*. To be sure, a strong personal element is unavoidable in respect of the ends and means of research as well as in the way the problems are conceived, but the views that are offered here are not subjective: they are objective, being based on arguments. They represent, not mere belief, but substantiated reasoning.

2. Our presentation is *not exclusive*. It attempts to do justice to all sides of linguistics. The fact that a science is adopting new points of view does not mean, as laymen may perhaps occasionally believe, that for that reason it rejects all previously obtained results as dispensable or even regrettable. Although Tycho Brahe erroneously assumed that the sun revolves around the earth, it does not follow that his observations, discoveries, and results have to be abandoned, but only that they have to be *reinterpreted*, converted according to the requirements of the newer point of view, and understood in a different way. The same holds true of those fields within classical linguistics where true observations and discoveries were made. In science it is quite possible to speak of permanent results—although hardly of permanent points of view. Nineteenth-century classical linguistics did achieve permanent results as regards the genetic relationship of languages, results that constitute an essential

side of linguistics. They will be presented here, however, in adjustment to new points of view, and they will be looked at somewhat differently from the way in which they perhaps were seen at the time of their discovery, so that the following account will differ in its principles from what is usually found in the handbooks on the subject.

Such an adjusted presentation of the main results of nineteenth-century linguistics will be our starting point, because the field to which they belong—the study of genetic relationship of languages—is still the best cultivated within the whole science of linguistics and because it is the only one for which classical linguistics produced what we can call—at least after reinterpretation—an exact method. This cornerstone of nineteenth-century classicism is also what gave rise to the critical approach of modern linguistics, and it will be used accordingly to introduce the reader to the modern framework within which problems of linguistic structure and linguistic change are treated.

# Linguistic Function

We gain insight into language, acquaintance with it, understanding or comprehension of it, in the same way as we gain insight into other objects—through a description. And to describe an object can mean only one thing: to give an account of the relationships into which it enters or which enter into it. Such relationships, or dependences, registered by a scientific description, we shall call *functions*. Thus we can describe a given object in two ways: (1) by dividing it into parts with mutual function, or *analyzing* it; (2) by placing it within a whole whose parts have mutual function, or *synthesizing* it. In the first case, the object is itself viewed as a functional whole; in the second, it is viewed as a part of a larger functional whole.

Accordingly, when the object we wish to describe is a language, we may

1. on the one hand, analyze the language into parts with mutual function; this is done in that kind of linguistics called *grammar*, which views the individual language (more precisely, the individual *état de langue*) as a closed totality and describes it by analyzing it and accounting for the functions between its parts;

2. on the other hand, place the language within a larger whole, i.e. view it as part of a *class of languages* and then describe the class by analyzing it and accounting for the functions between its parts.

The connexions between languages belonging to one and the same class of languages—or, in other words, the functions that establish a linguistic class—constitute *linguistic relationship*, of which we distinguish two kinds:

1. *genetic* relationship, which is found between languages belonging to the same *language family* and which points to a common origin for them;

2. *typological* relationship, which is found between languages belonging to the same *language type*; typological relationship does not point to a common origin, but is based on an agreement in structural features that is conditioned by the general possibilities of language.

In what follows we shall come to see what sorts of functions establish these two kinds of language classes, the language families and the language types. We shall also have occasion to determine some of the most important internal functions of the état de langue. Actually, of course, the analysis of the individual état de langue is a prerequisite for the classification of languages, but the chief problem of linguistics will always be, not the individual état de langue, but the relationship between different stages of a single language and between different languages, their similarities and their differences. This chief problem will therefore be attacked directly, while questions concerning the état de langue will be discussed as they arise and require elucidation in the course of the exposition.

# Genetic Relationship
# of Languages

Our own language belongs to the family usually called *Indo-European* (so named because it includes languages of both India and Europe). In what follows, a few examples of words from this family will be given to illustrate genetic relationship. If these examples have been chosen from the Indo-European family and not, as they might just as well have been, from some other, this is not only because the Indo-European family includes particularly well known languages (though whether the languages cited are known to the reader or not will be of no importance for his understanding the argument) and because our language belongs to it, but because, of all language families, it has been the most thoroughly studied and has been traced through the longest period of evolution and the broadest geographical diffusion. We know Indo-European languages over a period of 3500 years, and Indo-European languages are now spoken by 1.4 billion people, about half the world's population. By choosing this family as an example, we can demonstrate that our method is subject to no limitations of time or space.

On the other hand, we shall wish to choose our examples from among the many available so as to present our material in the simplest possible form and so as to avoid unnecessary complications that might at first obscure the general picture. In order to satisfy those two requirements—demonstration over a great extent of time and space, and simplicity of exposition—we shall choose our examples from certain Indo-European languages which (for reasons that can be discussed later) are particularly well suited to the purpose. The choice of languages will vary slightly from one example to another, but in the main we shall be using the languages listed in the following paragraph.

Among the languages having closest genetic relationship to our own, we shall usually choose *Gothic* (Goth.), which was spoken from about the year 200 to about the year 500 in large areas of Europe, from Spain in the West to the Crimea in the East, and into which the Bible was translated in the fourth century, in what is now Bulgarian territory. Only when a word is not attested in Gothic (i.e. not found in the extant Gothic texts) will we choose other closely related languages instead: *Old Norse* (ON), the language of the Icelandic sagas and the Norwegian Eddas; *Old High German* (OHG); or *Old English* (OE). To represent the Celtic languages we shall use either *Irish* (Ir.) or *Welsh*. Further, we shall cite *Latin* (Lat.), *Greek* (Gr.), *Lithuanian* (Lith.), *Old Church Slavic* (OCS), *Armenian* (Arm.), and *Old Indic* (OI)—and in some cases *Hittite* (Hitt.), an ancient language of Asia Minor that is known from a large number of cuneiform inscriptions, and *Tokharian* (Tokh.), a dead language preserved in manuscripts found in Chinese Turkestan. Further information about these and other related languages is not needed at the moment, but will be given in the chapter on language families.

We shall now first look at the words *brother*, *mother*, and *father*.

Our word *brother* is here cited from all the languages named above, excepting only Hittite:

| | | |
|---|---|---|
| Goth. *broþar* | Gr. *phrā́tōr, phrā́tēr* | Arm. *ełbayr* |
| Ir. *bráthir* | Lith. *broter-ĕlis* | OI. *bhrā́tā* |
| Lat. *frāter* (cf. Eng. fraternize) | OCS *bratrъ* | Tokh. *pracarə* |

Note:

1. So far as the individual letters of the transcriptions are concerned, it is enough for our purpose if the reader is able to recognize them when he meets them again later. Beyond that,

he need not be concerned with these oddities or try to imagine the pronunciation of the words cited. The following notes may serve to satisfy a natural curiosity, however: *þ* is pronounced like *th* in Eng. *thing*; a horizontal stroke over a vowel indicates that it is long; *l* is pronounced like *l* with the back of the tongue raised ("dark" *l*); *ə* is pronounced like *a* in Eng. *sofa*; OCS *ъ* is an extra-short vowel; Lith. *ė* is a long close *e* (like the first vowel in Ger. *Seele*), and the circumflex (˜) indicates a special intonation; Tokh. *c* is pronounced like *ch* in Eng. *child*.

2. The Lithuanian form is a hypocoristic and therefore supplied with a suffix *-ĕlis*, which we do not find in the words cited from the other languages. Another word for 'brother' in Lithuanian is *brólis* (where the acute accent indicates a special intonation different from the circumflex), which, although related to our word *brother*, is not identical with it.

3. The word means 'brother' in all the languages except literary Greek, where it has the special meaning '(fellow-)clansman', but we know that the same word in the Ionic dialect (where it has the slightly different form *phrḗtēr*) did mean 'brother'. In common Greek, 'brother' is *adelphós*, which is a different word. A 'clan', i.e. 'brotherhood', in Greek is *phrātría*, a derivative of the word *brother* which we also find in OCS *bratrija* and OI *bhrātryam*.

Our word *mother* is not preserved in Gothic (in the Gothic Bible, 'mother' appears as *aiþei*, which must be a different word), but we can cite:

| | | |
|---|---|---|
| ON *móðir* | Gr. *mā́tēr* (Attic *mḗtēr*) | Arm. *mayr* |
| Ir. *máthir* | Lith. *mótė, motẽ* 'woman', | OI *mātá* |
| Lat. *māter* | *mótina* 'mother' | Tokh. *mācarə* |
| | OCS *mati* | |

(Unless otherwise noted, the word in each language means 'mother'. Pronunciation: *ð* like *th* in Eng. *there*; Ir. *th* like *th* in Eng. *thing*.)

Our word *father* is not found in Lithuanian or Old Church

Slavic: the Lithuanian word for 'father' is *tĕvas*, which may perhaps be very distantly related to our word *father* but in any case is not identical with it; the Old Church Slavic is *otьcь*, a completely different word. Nevertheless, we can cite the following words, all meaning 'father':

Goth. *fadar*　　　　　　　Tokh. *pācarə*
Ir. *athir*　　　　　　　　Gr. *patĕr*
Lat. *pater* (cf.　　　　　Arm. *hayr*
　　Eng. *paternity*)　　　OI *pitá*

We shall now turn our attention to the *expression elements* composing these words in the different languages. These expression elements are represented in writing by letters, and in spoken language by speech sounds. (In some cases we use a combination of letters to represent one expression element: Ir. *th*, Gr. *ph*, and OI *bh* will be counted as representing one expression element each.) If we disregard the accents (which, of course, are also expression elements), the Greek words *phrátēr*, *mátēr*, and *patér*, for example, will be found to contain six, five, and five expression elements respectively.

Now it can be shown that between each expression element (EE) in one language and each EE in another, genetically related language there is a fixed dependence or relationship, or, as we have agreed to call it, a function. It is, in fact, on this function between the EE's of the different languages, on this *element-function*, that genetic relationship between languages rests. Incidentally, it is also due to this element-function that we often find, in such examples as the foregoing, a resemblance between words in different languages (although this need not be present—it would hardly be said that the Armenian words bear a very great "resemblance" to the others).

An especially simple case is the first EE in the word *mother*, which appears as *m* in all the languages we have cited. Now what is interesting and crucial is the possibility of establishing a rule that each time we have an *m* at the beginning of a syllable in a word in one of these languages, we have an *m* in the same word in all the other languages, provided the word is found in them. To be sure, such a rule is not without its restrictions, but these restrictions can be stated quite definitely and kept separate. We shall return to this question later, in our discussion of sign formation. First of all, we shall demonstrate the correctness of our rule by means of some examples:

*mouse*: ON *mús*, Lat. *mūs*, Gr. *mûs*, Arm. *mukn*, OI *mūḥ*.

*moon*, with its derivative, *month*: Goth. *mena* 'moon', *menops* 'month'; Ir. *mí* 'month'; Lat. *mēnsis* 'month'; Gr. *mḗn* 'month', *mēnē* 'moon'; Lith. *mḗnuo* 'moon', *mḗnesis* 'month'; OCS *měsęcъ* 'moon, month'; Arm. *amis* 'month'; OI *māḥ* 'moon, month'. (OCS *ě* pronounced approximately like *a* in Eng. *man*; *ę* like *in* in Fr. *fin*; *c* like *ts*; *ъ* an extra-short vowel different from *ъ*; OI *ḥ* is an ordinary *h* originating from *s*.)

*me*: Goth. *mi-k*, Welsh *mi*, Lat. *mē*, Gr. *me*, *emé*, *emé-ge*, Lith. *manè*, OCS *mę*, OI *mā*.

*murder*: Goth. *maurþr* 'murder'; Lat. *mors* 'death'; Gr. *mortós* 'mortal'; Lith. *mirtìs* 'death'; OCS *sъ-mrъtъ* 'death'; Arm. *mard* 'a man' (a mortal); OI *mṛtiḥ* 'death'. (*ṛ* indicates a syllabic *r*.)

'*winter*': ON *gimbr* 'yearling (one-winter-old) ewe lamb' (cf. dialectal Eng. *gimmer*); Ir. *gemred* 'winter'; Lat. *hiems* 'winter'; Gr. *kheîma* 'winter frost'; Lith. *žiemà* 'winter'; OCS *zima* 'winter'; Arm. *jmeṙn* 'winter'; OI *himáḥ* 'frost, snow', *himā* 'winter', *héman* 'in winter'; Hitt. *kimanza* 'winter'. (*ž* pronounced like *j* in Fr. *jour*; Hitt. *z=ts*; Arm. *j=dz*; Arm. *ṙ* is a strongly trilled apical *r*.)

*tame*: Goth. *ga-tamjan* 'to tame'; ON *tamr* 'tame', *temja* 'to tame'; Ir. *damnaim* 'I tie, I tame'; Lat. *domāre* 'to tame'; Gr. *damân* 'to tame'; OI *dāmyati* 'he tames, is tame'.

When *m* stands at the end of a syllable, it again appears as *m* in most of the languages, but in Old Church Slavic it combines with the preceding vowel to produce a nasal vowel. Starting from the meaning 'serrate', we can identify our word *comb*, ON *kambr* 'comb, crest, jagged beach', with Gr. *gómphos* 'bolt, dowel', OI *jámbhaḥ* (*j* pronounced as in English), Lith. *žaṁbas* 'uneven edge'. In Old Church Slavic the same word is *zǫbъ* 'tooth'. Such will be the case in all examples where *m* stands at the end of an internal syllable. The relationship is again different when the *m* stands at the end of a word: then, in Lithuanian we find a nasal vowel (no longer pronounced as a nasal in the standard language); in Old Church Slavic, we sometimes find nasalization of the vowel and sometimes zero, depending on certain prosodic conditions; in Greek we find -*n*; and in Gothic and Old Norse we find zero. Thus the word that we have just cited in the nominative case will, in the accusative (Indo-European ending -*m*), assume the following forms: OI *jámbham*, Lith. *žaṁbą*, OCS *zǫbъ*, Gr. *gómphon*, ON *kamb*. If the word had existed in Latin, the accusative form would have ended in -*m*, like other accusatives.

We thus find a constant function between the EE's of these languages, such that the same correspondences always appear under the same conditions. Using the symbol $\varphi$ to designate this constant dependence or function, we can state that under the first condition— syllable-initial position—we have:

Goth. *m* $\varphi$ Celt. *m* $\varphi$ Lat. *m* $\varphi$ Lith. *m* $\varphi$ OCS *m* $\varphi$ Arm. *m* $\varphi$ OI *m*.

But it would be rather cumbersome to write or to say all this every time we wished to refer to such an element-function between all the Indo-European languages, and for that reason, we use a more convenient system in which a single function through all the languages is designated by a single sign. Naturally, this sign—like all scientific symbols—is chosen quite arbitrarily. We could, if we wished, agree to use $x$ or $y$ or $z$ to refer to the whole long functional formula above. But the signs used in scientific formulæ are chosen not only arbitrarily, but also appropriately, and so, from purely practical considerations, we shall choose a formula that will directly recall to us something of what it is intended to designate. In the example before us, there can be no doubt that the simplest thing will be to choose the letter *m*, before which we shall set an asterisk to indicate that it is a formula for an element-function. Thus, instead of saying each time "agreement between Gothic *m*, Celtic *m*, Latin *m*, etc., at the beginning of a syllable," we shall say "Indo-European *m*" and write "IE *\*m*."

Besides arbitrariness and appropriateness, scientific formulæ have the additional property of simplicity. When we set about studying all the element-functions between the Indo-European languages and face the task of registering them, we shall prefer to use as few symbols as possible. To continue with our same example, we find that the conditions under which the function is different (syllable-final and word-final position) and the conditions under which our first function holds (syllable-initial position) are mutually exclusive. This being so, we can allow ourselves to use the same symbol in all these cases without running the risk of confusion. And since there are still languages where the EE concerned is represented by *m* in syllable-final and word-final positions, we can still use the symbol *\*m* and set up the equations

IE *\*m* = Goth. ON *m* $\varphi$ Gr. *m* $\varphi$ Lith. *m* $\varphi$ OCS ⳑ $\varphi$ OI *m*

in syllable-final position within the word, and

IE *\*-m* = Goth. ON Ø $\varphi$ Lat. *-m* $\varphi$ Gr. *-n* $\varphi$ Lith. ⳑ $\varphi$ OCS Ø (⳽) $\varphi$ OI *-m*.

In the latter formula we have even been able to state the condition (word-final position) simply by placing a hyphen before the *m*.

We do the same for all EE's, one by one, remembering to make do with the fewest possible Indo-European formulæ and therefore to bring together under a single formula as many different conditions as possible. The method is purely mechanical and easy to apply so long as the lexical material is available. Thus, the final element in *brother*, *mother*, and *father* can be identified with the second element in *brother* and denoted by the formula *\*r*. The reader can easily see from the given examples—to which many others could be added—that most of the languages under most conditions have a corresponding *r*, although in word-final position Lithuanian and Old Indic have zero. This zero will, of course, be in turn replaced by *r* when we change the conditions—that is, when we introduce into the same word, so far as that is possible, the conditions under which the language concerned has a corresponding *r*: in the accusative, Old Indic has *bhrā́tar-am*, *mātár-am*, *pitár-am* and Lithuanian has *móter-į*; cf. also Lith. *broter-ĕlis*.

The same examples (and, again, many more could be added) make it immediately obvious that the third EE in *brother* and the second EE in *mother* are identical and can be formulated as

IE *\*ā* = Goth. *o*, ON *ó* φ Ir. *á* φ Lat. *ā* φ Gr. *ā* (*ē*) φ Lith. *o* φ OCS *a* φ Arm. *a* φ OI *ā* φ Tokh. *ā* (*a*).

IE *\*ā* can also appear at the end of a word, but under this condition it corresponds to other functional formulæ. We have already seen examples of this: since *\*-ā* is a feminine nominative ending (cf. the Latin first declension, in *-a*), it is found in a large number of words, including those we have cited above as OI *himā* 'winter', Lith. *žiemà*, OCS *zima*, and Gr. *mḗnē* 'moon', which would be *mḗnā* in dialects other than Attic and Ionic. On this basis we can conclude:

IE *\*-ā* = Lat. *-a* φ Gr. *-ā* (*-ē*) φ Lith. *-a* φ OCS *-a* φ OI *-ā*.

The second EE in *father* reveals the function

Goth. *a* φ Ir. *a* φ Lat. *a* φ Gr. *a* φ Arm. *a* φ OI *i* φ Tokh. *ā*,

which we sum up in the symbol IE *\*A* (reserving *\*a* for the cases where OI *a* corresponds to *a* of the other languages, as in OI *ájati* 'drives', Arm. *acem* 'I lead, bring', Gr. *ágein* 'to lead', Lat. *agere* 'to drive, lead', Ir. *agat* 'let them lead', ON *aka* 'to drive'). This correspondence holds only for the first syllable of a word;

other syllables show other element-functions corresponding to IE *ᴀ.

Let us conclude this sampling of element-functions by taking a closer look at the first EE in the word *father* and the third EE from the end in the words *brother*, *mother*, and *father*. For the former we shall write IE *$p$, and for the latter, IE *$t$.

The word *father* displays the function

IE *$p$ = Goth. *f* φ Ir. Ø φ Lat. *p* φ Gr. *p* φ Arm. *h* φ OI *p* φ Tokh. *p*,

a function that we find in an enormous number of other examples, some of which also show us that the Hittite correspondence is *p*. We shall cite a few of these:

*feather*: ON *fjǫdr*, OHG *fedara* 'feather'; OHG *fed(a)rah* 'wing'; Ir. *én* 'bird'; Old Welsh *eterin* 'bird'; Lat. *petere* 'to seek, strive for, make for, travel to'; Gr. *pétesthai* 'fly, rush'; OI *pátati* 'it flies', *pátram* 'wing'; Hitt. *pítaizi* 'flees', *pítar* 'wing'.

*fish*: Goth. *fisks*, Middle Ir. *iasc*, Lat. *piscis* (in Slavic, Pol. *piskorz* 'loach', Russ. *piskar'* 'gudgeon'). (Lat. *c* pronounced like *k*.)

ME *fee* 'cattle, property': Goth. *faihu* 'property, money'; ON *fé* 'cattle, money, property'; Lat. *pecu*, *pecus* 'cattle', *pecūnia* 'wealth, money' (cf. Eng. *pecuniary*); OI *páśu*, *paśú*, *paśúḥ* 'cattle'.

Dan. *(i)fjor* 'last year': ON *fjǫðr*, Gr. (Doric) *péruti*, Lith. *pérnai*, Arm. *heru*, OI *parút*.

The conditions for this function turn out to be quite restricted, when we consider all the languages participating in it. In Armenian, for example, we do not find *h*, but zero, when *$p$ stands word-initially before IE *$o$ (thus, Arm. *otn* corresponds to Eng. *foot*, Goth. *fotus*, Gr. *poús*). But under most conditions this function is found at the beginning of words. In the group *$sp$, we find *p* in all the languages, including Gothic; so, for example, ON *spá* 'to foretell', OHG *spehōn* 'to spy', as compared with Lat. *specere, spectāre, īn-spicere* 'to inspect', *haru-spex* 'augur (who *inspects* the victim's entrails for omens)'. But within the word, *\*p* corresponds to quite different functions, as we shall see shortly.

The EE function Goth. ON *f* φ Lat. Gr. *þ* was first recognized by Rasmus Rask, in 1814 (in his prize essay entitled *Investigation on the Origin of the Old Norse or Icelandic Language*), in connexion with a whole set of other EE functions holding for word-initial position in the same languages, like Goth. ON *t* φ Lat. Gr. *d*, of which we have seen an example in the word *tame*. For this latter function (and corresponding functions under other conditions) we establish the formula IE *\*d*, and from our example of *tame*, supplemented by appropriate material from Lithuanian, Old Church Slavic, and Armenian, we can read off the following function:

IE *\*d* = Goth. ON *t* φ Ir. *d* φ Lat. *d* φ Gr. *d* φ Lith. *d* φ OCS *d* φ Arm. *t* φ OI *d*.

We find good examples for this function in the numerals *two* and *ten*:

Goth. *twai*, Ir. *dáu*, Lat. *duo*, Gr. *dúo*, Lith. *dù*, OCS *dъva*, OI *dvau*.

Goth. *taihun*, Ir. *deich*, Lat. *decem*, Gr. *déka*, Lith. *dēšimt*, OCS *desętъ*, Arm. *tasn*, OI *dáśa*. (*š* pronounced like Eng. *sh*.)

The set of word-initial EE functions recognized by Rask also includes the function for *\*t*: Goth. ON *þ* φ Lat. Gr. *t*, or, more fully:

Goth. ON *þ* φ Celt. *t* φ Lat. *t* φ Gr. *t* φ Lith. *t* φ OCS *t* φ Arm. *th* φ OI *t*,

as exemplified by:

*thirst*: Goth. *þaursus* 'dry', *þaurstei* 'thirst', *þaursjan* 'to thirst', *ga-þairsan, ga-þaursnan* 'to dry up'; Ir. *tart* 'thirst'; Lat. *torridus* 'dry', *torrēre* 'to dry up, roast, bake'; Gr. *térsesthai*

'to become dry', *tersáinein* 'to dry', *trasiá, tarsiá, tarsós*
'drying crate'; Arm. *thaṙ* 'rod for drying grapes'; OI *tṛṣyati*
'is thirsty', *tarṣaḥ* 'thirst', *tṛṣṭáḥ* 'dry, hoarse'. (*ṣ* and *ṭ* pronounced with the tip of the tongue turned back to the roof of
the mouth.)

*thin*: ON *þunnr*, Ir. *tanae*, Lat. *tenuis*, Gr. *tanaós* 'long', OCS
*tьnъkъ* 'thin, slender', OI *tanúḥ, tánukaḥ*. (The meaning is
'thin' unless otherwise indicated.)

This functional formula holds for word-initial position before
a vowel. Under other conditions, word-initial *\*t* will have other
representations in some of the languages, but in Gothic and Old
Norse it is always represented by *þ*. In the group *\*st*, Gothic
and Old Norse have *t*, just as they have *p* for *\*p* in *\*sp*; compare Goth. *steigan* 'to climb up' and Gr. *steíkhein* 'to walk,
march'.

But as we can see by the third EE from the end in *brother,
mother,* and *father*, there are functions for *\*t* within the word that
differ from what we find in word-initial position; moreover, we
observe that Gothic has different representatives in *broþar* and
*fadar*, corresponding to a single representative in the other
languages. The conditions must therefore be different in the
two words. If we collect the examples for this contrast, we find
that what decides whether we shall find *þ* or *d* in Gothic is the
place of the accent in the corresponding Old Indic word. If the
word accent in Old Indic immediately precedes the *t*, Gothic
has *þ*, otherwise *d*; thus *broþar* corresponds to OI *bhrā́tā*, but
*fadar* to OI *pitā́*. This relationship between Gothic consonants
and Indic accent was discovered by the Danish linguist Karl
Verner in 1876. We have already stated (p. 13) that the accents
must be counted among the expression elements; Verner's law
implies, of course, that the Old Indic accents must be included
in our Indo-European formulæ.

It turns out, as a matter of fact, that accent relationships
(or, at least, phenomena that appear to us most directly in the
form of accent relationships) play a role in the EE functions in

many other respects. It has been shown that the Greek opposition between circumflex (ˆ) and acute (ˊ) accentuation of the accented syllable is also found or reflected in many other Indo-European languages (most clearly in Lithuanian, where ˜, on the one hand, and ˊ or ˋ, on the other, are distributed in final syllables as are ˆ and ˊ in Greek). The formula given above (p. 17) for IE *-ā holds only when the *-ā stands, in Greek and Lithuanian, in the kind of syllable that takes the acute when accented (and this is precisely the case for the ending of the feminine nominative). When *-ā stands in the kind of syllable that takes the circumflex when accented in Greek and Lithuanian, we obtain another function. In such cases, Lithuanian has *o*, not *a*, corresponding to IE *-ā, as in the feminine genitive ending represented by Gr. -ās (-ēs) and Lith. -os.

We have thus found a relationship between the Indo-European languages under consideration such that a given EE in one language, in the environment of other given EE's and in a given place in the word, has a constant correspondence to a given EE in each of the other languages. And this relationship can be demonstrated for all EE's in all Indo-European languages. Thus the whole EE-system in each of the languages stands in a constant relationship to the whole EE-system in each of the other languages. It is this constant correspondence that we call the EE-function or *element-function* (provided we agree to understand this latter term as referring to *expression* elements).

The principle behind this observation can be generalized. It is universal: wherever there is genetic relationship between languages, there is element-function between their systems. This is true of all language families, far and near, small and large. In those instances where it has been possible to establish genetic relationship between American Indian languages, the very same method has been used. When we establish, or try to establish, genetic relationship between Indo-European and other languages, it is again a matter of establishing element-function. And element-function is also used to establish the kind of closer relationships found within subfamilies. For a large language family like Indo-European contains subfamilies for which we can establish specific element-functions and set up corresponding formulæ. In other words, there are language families within language families, or language families of different degrees.

One subfamily within Indo-European is *Italic*, which includes Latin and the modern *Romance* languages (Italian, Spanish, French, Rumanian, etc.). Here is one example of an element-function between the Romance languages:

$*ct$ = It. *tt* $\varphi$ Sp. *ch* (pronounced like Eng. *ch*) $\varphi$ Fr. *it* $\varphi$ Rum. *pt*,

as in:

| It. *fatto* | Sp. *hecho* | Fr. *fait* | Rum. *fapt* | 'done' |
| It. *latte* | Sp. *leche* | Fr. *lait* | Rum. *lapte* | 'milk' |
| It. *notte* | Sp. *noche* | Fr. *nuit* | Rum. *noapte* | 'night' |

Just as we called our formulæ Indo-European when we were comparing the Indo-European languages, so the Romanists give their formulæ a name, calling them Common Romance, Proto-Romance, or Vulgar Latin. From considerations of appropriateness, these are chosen so as to resemble as much as possible the corresponding EE's in Latin as it has come down to us. But they are just as arbitrary as the Indo-European formulæ, and there are many instances where it would be impossible to bring them into agreement with the EE's in the Latin words.

Another subfamily within Indo-European is *Germanic* (Gmc.), which includes Gothic, Old Norse and the other Scandinavian languages, and the several stages of German and English. Its formulæ are called Common Germanic or Proto-Germanic, and it turns out to be appropriate to choose them so that in many (but not all) cases they will resemble the EE's of Gothic. Thus, for example, the Germanist has no need of starting from IE $*t$, but can set up a Gmc. $*þ$ and show which functions between the Germanic languages correspond to it under different conditions.

For the condition illustrated by the examples given above, we obtain the following function:

Gmc. *þ* = Goth. þ φ ON þ φ Modern Scand. (Dan., Swed., Nor.) *t* φ OE þ φ Modern Eng. *th* (voiceless, as in *thin*) φ HG *d*.

Citing the languages in this order, and returning to our old examples from this new point of view, we find:

Goth. *þaursus*, etc.; ON *þurr* 'dry', *þerra*, *þorna* 'to dry', *þorsti* 'thirst', *þyrstr* 'thirsty'; Dan. *tør* 'dry', *tørre* 'to dry', *tørst* 'thirst'; OE *þyrre* 'dry', *þurst* 'thirst'; Modern Eng. *thirst*; OHG *durri* 'dry' *derren*, *dorrên* 'to dry', *durst* 'thirst'; Modern HG *dürr* 'dry', *dorren* 'to be dried', *dörren* 'to dry', *Durst* 'thirst'.
ON *þunnr* 'thin', Dan. *tynd*, Modern Eng. *thin*, OHG *dunni*, Modern HG *dünn*.

In corresponding fashion, we can set up Gmc. *t*, from the Germanic point of view, for the examples used above to set up IE *d*:

Gmc. *t* = Goth. *t* φ ON *t* φ Modern Scand. *t* φ OE *t* φ Modern Eng. *t* φ HG z,

as in

Goth. *ga-tamjan*, ON *tamr*, *temja*, Dan. *tam*, *tamme*, OE *tam*, *temian*, Modern Eng. *tame*, OHG *zam*, *zamôn*, *zemmen*, Modern HG *zahm*, *zähmen*.
Goth. *twai*, ON *tveir*, Dan. *to*, Modern Eng. *two*, OHG *zwêne*, Modern HG *zwei*.
Goth. *taihun*, ON *tíu*, Dan. *ti*, OE *tíen*, Modern Eng. *ten*, OHG *zehan*, Modern HG *zehn*.

The EE-functions HG *d* φ Goth. ON *þ* and HG z φ Goth. ON *t* were recognized in 1814 by Rask, in the essay already mentioned, in connexion with some other EE-functions for the same languages. Just as Gmc. $f$ = IE *$p$ and Gmc. $þ$ = IE *$t$ are particularly striking and characteristic functions for Germanic in its relationship to the other Indo-European languages, so HG $d$ = Gmc. *$þ$ and HG $z$ = Gmc. *$t$ are particularly striking and characteristic functions for High German in its relationship to the other Germanic languages. (Low German has *th* (later *d*) and *t* respectively: in Old Saxon—the old form of Low German—'thin' is *thunni* and 'ten' is *tehan*. This is one of the most immediately striking differences between the two languages of Germany, High German and Low German.) These characteristic High German functions also include $t$ = Gmc. *$d$ (Goth. *d*), so that Verner's opposition of Goth. *broþar* and *fadar* takes the form in High German of an opposition between $d$ and $t$: *Bruder, Vater*.

Of course, a single EE in one language can correspond to two or more different EE's in the related languages. We have seen above (p. 17) both OI *i* and OI *a* in the first syllable of words as corresponding EE's to *a* in the other languages, where *a* therefore equals IE *$A$ in some words and IE *$a$ in others. As we can see, a distinction found in one language may be obliterated in another. Thus, Verner's distinction between Goth. *broþar* and *fadar*, Modern HG *Bruder* and *Vater*, which is also found in OE *bróþor*, *fæder*, is obliterated both in Scandinavian (Icelandic *bróðir*, *faðir*, Dan. *broder*, *fader*) and in Modern English (*brother*, *father*) since these languages have in this case only one EE corresponding to both Gmc. *$þ$ and Gmc. *$d$. Another such case to be found in our examples is that of Dan. (Modern Scand.) *t*, which in some words (like *tør* 'dry' and *tynd* 'thin') corresponds to Gmc. *$þ$, IE *$t$, and in others (like *tam* 'tame', *to* 'two', and *ti* 'ten') to Gmc. *$t$, IE *$d$. Thus, genetically related languages by no means need have the same number of EE's or the same system of EE's.

The subfamilies of which we have seen examples stand within the great Indo-European language family as states within a state. They are established according to the very same principle as the great family, but independently of it. The Germanist, or Romanist, can work within a closed system in which the Germanic, or Romance, formulæ are adequate tools, without having to look beyond the limits of the subfamily to the other members of the larger family. This fact determines a useful division of labor among the linguists engaged in the study of genetic relationship. Each language family, however small, as well as each part of a language family, is like a microcosm, organized in exactly the same way as the larger families. For example, we could consider the Scandinavian languages apart from the rest and establish a set of common formulæ just for them. We could restrict our domain even further, taking the East Scandinavian languages (Danish and Swedish) by themselves and treating them in quite the same way. And we could even take the Danish dialects by themselves and show how they have mutual element-functions that can be accounted for by a Common Danish system of formulæ. From this point of view, each domain is sufficient to itself. By selecting certain element-functions as peculiarly characteristic of a given language group, a given language, or a given dialect area (like the consonantal functions that we found to be specifically peculiar to High German, opposing it to all the other Germanic languages), we are led to distinguish language families of different degrees or of different size. And generally it is, of course, most expedient to stay within as narrowly restricted a family as possible when treating its internal problems. The Danish dialects are accounted for from Common Danish, Danish from East Scandinavian, and East Scandinavian from Scandinavian (or Norse). Further, if we follow the classification of the Germanic languages proposed on pp. 70–71, Scandinavian will be accounted for from East Germanic, East Germanic from Germanic, Germanic from Indo-European, and Indo-European from common formulæ for functions between Indo-European and non–Indo-European languages. It is this continuous gradation that determined the choice of languages (p. 11) to be used in exhibiting some of the Indo-European element-functions. We could, of course, compare Danish directly with Latin, or French with Old Indic, but such comparisons introduce complications that can be avoided if we first choose a Germanic language that is closer to Common Germanic than Danish, or an Italic language that is closer to Common Italic than French. Without an intermediate link, we should face the complications of having to account for all the instances where Danish obliterates a distinction found in Common Germanic or in Gothic, or where Danish introduces a difference that is not found there, or, correspondingly, where French obliterates a distinction found in Common Italic or in Latin, or introduces a distinction that is not found there.

Thus, for every language family, large or small, the linguist uses as his tools a set or system of common formulæ in which he summarizes the observed element-functions in the simplest and most economical way. Each language family can be accounted for from its system, and each period in the history of linguistic research has had its own system for each family, since further simplifications are often possible. For example, in the course of the last hundred-odd years at least three clearly different systems, each with its own nuances, have been set up for Indo-European. The third one is even now in the course of formation, and we shall discuss it a little later. In this section we have provisionally kept to a methodological exposition of the system arrived at by classical linguistics, that is to say, the second of the three. In summary, this system has the following aspects:

1. *Consonants*, i.e. entities that do not by themselves establish a syllable. Of these, we set up a minimum of $5 \times 4 + 3 = 23$:

| | | | |
|---|---|---|---|
| $*p$ | $*ph$ | $*b$ | $*bh$ |
| $*t$ | $*th$ | $*d$ | $*dh$ |
| $*k_1$ | $*k_1h$ | $*g_1$ | $*g_1h$ |
| $*k_2$ | $*k_2h$ | $*g_2$ | $*g_2h$ |
| $*k_3$ | $*k_3h$ | $*g_3$ | $*g_3h$ |
| $*s$ | $*þ$ | $*j$ | |

2. *Vowels*, i.e. entities that by themselves establish a syllable. Of these, we set up a minimum of $2 \times 3 = 6$:

*a   *e   *o
*ā   *ē   *ō

3. The entity *A. (Classical theory counted this among the vowels; here, it is placed by itself in anticipation of later discoveries.)

4. *Coefficients*, i.e. entities that by themselves sometimes establish and sometimes do not establish a syllable. There are six of these, but they can appear both as syllable-forming and as non–syllable-forming, and, in the first case, both as short and long. When we take these possibilities into account, the total becomes $3 \times 6 = 18$:

| | | | | | | |
|---|---|---|---|---|---|---|
| syllable-forming short: | *i | *u | *r̥ | *l̥ | *n̥ | *m̥ |
| syllable-forming long: | *ī | *ū | *r̥̄ | *l̥̄ | *n̥̄ | *m̥̄ |
| non–syllable-forming: | *i̯ | *u̯ | *r | *l | *n | *m |

A combination of a vowel and a coefficient (e.g. *ai̯ *eu̯ *or *āl *ēn *ōm, etc.) is called a diphthong.

Each of these symbols, then, is an abbreviated formula for a set of functions that are present under mutually exclusive conditions. Obviously, there is nothing to prevent our using these symbols in combination when we need to indicate that the related languages have two or more combined EE's, each of which corresponds to a particular symbol in the system. Indeed, we have already done so in the case of the Indo-European diphthongs, which are just such combinations of symbols. We did the same on pp. 18 and 20 in operating with IE *sp and *st, and on p. 22 in operating with Common Romance *ct. And we can combine more symbols, as a matter of course, whenever we need to do so. We need not always do so; in fact, it quite rarely happens that a whole word or parts of a word are completely identical in the different languages ("identical" here means "capable of being registered as consisting of the same Indo-European entities"). If, for example, we look at the words for 'moon' and 'month', or at the words we have collected under the rubrics *me*, *murder*, and 'winter' (p. 14), we see that they are not identical in all respects: they have been formed according to the special rules of word formation in each language. Only certain components of each word, certain EE's, remain unchanged from language to language, and these are the ones that the linguist abstracts and uses as bases for his constructions. We saw above that the cited words all include an IE *\*m*, just as we observed (pp. 14, 19) that the words for 'tame' are identical in containing a representative of *\*m* and a representative of *\*d* in all the languages cited. Several of our illustrative words have been identical in respect of many other EE's—otherwise, they would not have served as evident examples for the nonspecialist. But in actual practice it is very seldom that we can trace a whole word through the entire Indo-European family and find it remaining fully identical with itself in all the languages. It happens, however, that *brother*, *mother*, and *father* can be traced as whole words, at least if we ignore the Greek variant *phrátōr*, with its divergent vowel in the last syllable, and Lithuanian *mótina*, which has an extension containing *n*. They can therefore be formulated in their entirety as IE *\*bhrátēr*, *\*mātér*, and *\*pAtér*. In the same way the Romanist can identify each set of words on p. 22 and represent them by the formulæ *\*factu*, *\*lacte*, *\*nocte*. On the other hand, once we have set up our whole system of formulæ, we may often find it useful to take a word appearing in a given language—perhaps, in that particular form, only in that language—and, on the basis of our general knowledge of the element-functions, to transpose it into an Indo-European formula. Obviously, nothing stands in the way of our doing so. We can say, for example, that while all the other forms of the word *brother* represent IE *\*bhrátēr*, Greek *phrátōr* is to be interpreted as IE *\*bhrátōr*. In this way we can take any word whatsoever in any Indo-European language whatsoever and "translate" it into an Indo-European formula.

We have said that words often differ somewhat in the different

Indo-European languages because they have been formed according to the special rules of word formation in each language, but this should not be taken to mean that the rules of word formation shift radically from one language to another. So long as we keep to the languages that can be most immediately accounted for by the Common Indo-European system of formulæ (Gothic, for example, rather than Modern Danish, Latin rather than French), we find, on the contrary, that word formation follows the same rules in all the languages, only that each language, for each individual word, enjoys a certain freedom of choice from among several common rules. That is to say, the system of formulæ for sets of EE-functions is not the only working tool that we can set up; in addition, we can have a system of rules of word formation that hold for all the languages being directly compared. The alternation between *ē* and *ō* that we have just now observed in the Greek word corresponding to English *brother* reflects part of just such a rule. A very important feature in the Indo-European rules of word formation consists of the so-called *vowel alternations*, according to which a certain vowel (or, as it is called, a certain alternation grade) will appear under certain grammatical conditions, depending also on relations of accent and on the alternation grade found in other syllables of the word. But these rules allow for a certain margin of variation, so that sometimes two alternation grades may appear in one and the same word. Moreover, the individual Indo-European languages make somewhat different application of the same rules. We shall not go into these here, but merely note that the most important vowel alternation in Indo-European is between *e*, *o*, *Ø*, *ē*, and *ō*. The Greek verb 'to fly' (see above, p. 18) has the *e*-grade between the *p* and the *t* in the present infinitive *pétesthai*, while the perfect has the *o*-grade (together with a prefixed reduplication syllable *pe*-), so that 'I have flown' is *pe-pót-ēmai*. Another past tense (the aorist) of the same verb has the zero grade, that is, no vowel between the *p* and the *t*: 'I flew' is *e-pt-ómēn*. When the vowel *e* is the first part of a diphthong, the alternation *e : *o : Ø will of course appear as an alternation *ei̯ : *oi̯ : *i, or *eu̯ : *ou̯ : *u, or *en : *on : *n̥, and so on. The vowel alternation that we find in English strong verbs depends on these Common Indo-European rules of word formation. Forms like *sing, sang, sung* contain, respectively, IE *en, *on, and *n̥ (*n̥ appears in Germanic as *un*).

From what has been said, we can conclude that *genetic relationship is a function between languages consisting in the fact that each expression element in each of the languages has function to an expression element in each of the other languages*; and we have seen that *each particular element-function is conditioned by the other expression elements forming the environment of the expression element concerned and by the place that it occupies in the word.*

This is what is called an *operational* definition: it is a definition that provides a criterion, a test to decide whether genetic relationship is present in a given case or not. As can be seen, the definition is based on the functions between the languages and on the functions between their expression elements. In itself, it has nothing to say about the kind of function connecting the expression elements of the different languages with the common formulæ—or about the kind of function connecting each of the languages with the system of the common formulæ. Although we have not yet closely examined the nature of this function, we shall nevertheless give it a name and call it a *continuation*; we shall say that the expression elements in each of the languages *continue* the common formulæ and that the system of each language—or, in general, that each language—*continues* the aggregate system of the common formulæ. And later on we shall be able to inquire into the meaning of such statements.

When, on p. 14, we began to set up element-functions, we made the general reservation that they do not hold without restrictions. The restrictions on the domains of the element-functions must be taken into account. They do not constitute *exceptions* to the element-functions, if by exceptions we understand arbitrary and irregular violations of a rule. They constitute *counter-examples*, i.e. strictly defined and strictly delimited regular domains for which the element-functions do not hold and which must therefore be excluded from our calculations before we establish the element-functions. The element-functions are like the Danish laws that are not promulgated for the Faeroe Islands. Once we know that fact, we can exclude the Faeroe Islands from consideration. Outside the Faeroe Islands, the law holds without exception; on the Faeroe Islands, other laws hold.

The counter-examples are never such that certain expression *elements* in a language are unaffected by the principle of the element-functions. We have already said that each expression element in a language contracts element-functions with one or more expression elements in the other languages. Thus it is always the entire system of the expression elements that is affected by the element-functions, and we never find any enclave, or any individual elements, within that system that we have to exclude from consideration. It is not merely certain elements in the one language that have function to certain elements in the other, but all to all; it is the one *linguistic structure* that has function to the other.

The counter-examples consist rather in the fact that certain *signs* (certain words, for example) in a language are not affected by the element-functions in the same way as other signs. We find certain kinds of signs (including certain kinds of words) whose elements do not contract the same element-functions as do the elements of other signs (other words), and we must therefore identify such special signs and exclude them from consideration when we are registering the element-functions. The counter-examples do not concern the elements as such, but only the signs composed by the elements and the functions contracted by these signs and their elements in the *linguistic usage*. Before we proceed to the counter-examples, therefore, it will be necessary to say a few words about element and sign, about the different kinds of functions between elements and between signs within one and the same language, and about linguistic structure and linguistic usage.

# Linguistic Structure
# and Linguistic Usage

Every language appears to us first of all as a system of *signs*, that is to say, a system of expression units that have content, or meaning, attached to them. Words are signs of this sort. But parts of words can also be signs: -*s* in English is a sign of the genitive (*Jack'-s father*) and a sign of the third person singular present (*he write-s*). A word like *in-act-iv-ate-s* is a sign consisting of five different smaller signs. A sign may consist of one expression element with one content element attached to it, like the English sign -*s* in *Jack's father*, which consists of the expression element *s* with its attached content element 'genitive'; or it may be formed—both on the expression side and on the content side—by the combination of two or more elements, like the Latin sign -*ārum* in *bon-ārum mulierum* 'of the good women', which consists of four expression elements—*ā*, *r*, *u*, and *m*—and three content elements—'genitive', 'plural', and 'feminine'.

When we look at a printed or written text, we see that it consists of signs and that these, in turn, consist of elements proceeding in a certain direction (Latin letters from left to right, Hebrew letters from right to left, Mongolian letters from top to bottom—but always in some definite direction). And when we hear a spoken text, we find that it consists of signs and that these, in turn, consist of elements proceeding in time—some come earlier and some later. The signs form *chains*, and the elements within each sign likewise form chains. We shall use the term *relation* for the function (dependence, relationship) between signs or between elements within one and the same chain: the signs, or the elements, are *related* to one another in the chain.

If we take as an example an English sign like the word *pat*, we can form other signs by inserting other elements in the place of each element within it. This is possible with regard to both the content elements and the expression elements, but we shall here confine ourselves to the latter, which are the more easily observed. Thus, we can replace each expression element in the sign *pat* with other expression elements to form such new signs as *sat, rat, tat*; *pet, pit, pot*; *pan, pad, pal*. We can set up the sign *pat* as a horizontal chain proceeding from left to right and then place under each of its elements, in a vertical column, other elements that could be inserted in its place:

| | | |
|---|---|---|
| *p* | *a* | *t* |
| *s* | *e* | *n* |
| *r* | *i* | *d* |
| *t* | *o* | *l* |
| . | . | . |
| . | . | . |

Such vertical columns we shall call *paradigms*. Thus, a paradigm of elements will mean a class of elements that can be inserted in one and the same place in a chain: *p a t* is a chain; *p s r t* is a paradigm. The function between the members of a paradigm we shall call a *correlation*. Between *p*, *a*, and *t* we have a relation; between *p*, *s*, *r*, and *t* we have a correlation.

Now the peculiar fact is that we cannot introduce just any elements into any paradigm. By doing so, we might (as we shall shortly be interested in observing) produce signs previously unused in English, like *miv* or *jeg*, which are still linguistically possible in the sense of being permitted by the rules governing element combinations in English, but we might also produce groups of elements, like *pgt*, or *pkt*, that would conflict with those rules. Although the elements are all right, they are combined incorrectly and the sign is impossible.

We can thus construct a paradigm consisting of elements that can be inserted only in certain places in the chain and not in others. We shall call such a paradigm a *category*. Thus, *a*, *e*, and *i* might belong to one category, and *g* and *k* to another.

When, however, we speak of restrictions on the formation of signs, we are making a very superficial observation based on our preliminary view of language as it first appears to us, as a system of signs. If we wish to penetrate more deeply and inquire what these restrictions in sign formation depend on, what structural peculiarity of language prevents a sign from having just any appearance whatsoever, we shall find the reason in the fact that there are certain rules for the construction of the syllable. There cannot be an English sign *pgt* or *pkt* for the following reasons:

1. There cannot be a syllable *pgt* or *pkt* in English. If there could be, then *pgt* and *pkt* might well be English signs, just as well as English *pat*, *pet*, and *pit*, or as *miv* and *jeg*, which are unused sign-possibilities in English but still sign-possibilities, precisely because they are formed in accordance with the English rules for syllable formation.

2. There cannot be a syllable in English ending in *-pgt* or *-pkt*. If there could be, then *pgt* and *pkt* might well be English signs—like *-s*, for example, which does not form a syllable by itself but which can be used as a sign in English because English syllables can end in *-s* (*cats*, *rats*, *hats*, etc.).

3. There cannot be a syllable in English beginning in *pgt-* or *pkt-*. If there could be, then it would be possible for *pgt* and *pkt* to be English signs, since in such a case they might always be used by being attached to the beginning of a syllable, as *-s* is always attached at the end.

4. There cannot be a syllable in English ending in *-pg* or *-pk*, or beginning in *gt-* or *kt-*. If there could be, then again it would be possible for *pgt* or *pkt* to be English signs; they would only have to be so used as always to include a syllable boundary: *apg-ta* or *ap-gta*, etc.

Thus we find that the sign-possibilities depend directly on the syllable-possibilities. The structure of language is not so ordered as to have special rules governing the shape of a *sign*. A sign may be a syllable (e.g. *pat*) or not (e.g. -*s*), and it may consist of one or more syllables (*category*, for example, consists of four). But there *are* special rules in the linguistic structure governing the shape of *syllables*, and signs must, of course, be so constructed as not to violate them.

Now what is a syllable? A syllable is not a sign (the word *category*, for example, consists of four syllables, but not of four signs). A syllable may quite accidentally coincide with a sign, since a sign may consist of one and only one syllable (as in the case of *pat*), but even then syllable and sign are not the same. The first part of *category* is the same syllable as *cat*, but not the same sign. A syllable is something different: it is a *unit of elements* resulting from the fact that certain elements contract relation with one another. The structure of the syllable depends on the relations that can be contracted by the elements—relations governed by special rules for each element or each category of elements. We said above that Eng. *a*, *e*, and *i* belong to one category and *g* and *k* to another. The category to which *a*, *e*, and *i* belong is called the category of *vowels*; the category to which *g* and *k* belong is called the category of *consonants*. Vowels each have the property of being able to form a syllable by themselves, while consonants do not. Vowels and consonants may contract relation with one another within a syllable, or combine to form a syllable. But there are certain restrictions on relations between vowel and vowel, and between consonant and consonant, within one and the same syllable. Not every element can be connected with every other, but only some with some. And the rules governing relations may be such that, for example, certain consonants may be combined in a certain order but not in all conceivable orders: an English syllable may end in -*pt* but not in -*tp*.

Thus each element in a language has its place in a certain category, which is defined by certain definite relational possibilities and which excludes certain others. All such categories, together with their definitions, constitute the element-system of the language, or what we call its *linguistic structure*. The linguistic structure determines which are possible syllables of the language and which are not—and hence, in turn, which are possible signs of the language and which are not.

It follows from the linguistic structure of English that we can form such syllables as *pat, sat, rat, pet, set, ret, pit, sit, rit, pan, san, ran, pen, sen, ren, pin, sin, rin, pad, sad, rad, ped, sed, red, pid, sid,* and *rid*. These, and others, can be read off from the little schema on p. 33. And, in fact, all these syllables are found in English words. Even so, a syllable derivable from the linguistic structure will not always be actually used. The linguistic structure permits the formation of English syllables beginning with *spr-*, but while such possibilities as *spring* and *sprat* are actually used, others, like *spreb* and *sprust*, are not. No rules can be set up to determine the use that is made of possibilities offered by the linguistic structure; whether a given possibility is used or rejected is a matter of pure chance.

Much the same is true of signs. Since a sign, like any other chain in the language, must conform to the rules of syllable formation found in the linguistic structure, it follows that certain sign formations are excluded. But it also follows that certain others are permitted. The chains *pat, sat, rat*, etc., cited above, are possible signs since they are possible syllables, but possible syllables can be found, like *pid* or *maf*, that are not signs in English. They are unused sign-possibilities, and the fact that they are not used, while certain others are, is pure accident. Moreover, we are free to use them any moment we wish. We can decide tomorrow to introduce an English word *pid* or *maf* with some meaning or another, and we can do so because they are possible syllables—the elements entering into them are given the possibility, in the linguistic structure, of occupying these places.

As we have said before, a language first appears to us as a system of signs. But we now see that in fact a language is primarily something different, namely a system of *elements* appointed to occupy certain definite places in the chain, to contract certain definite relations to the exclusion of certain others. These elements can be *used*, in conformity with the rules that govern them, to form signs. The number of elements and the relational possibilities of each element are laid down once and for all in the *linguistic structure*. Which of these possibilities will be exploited is determined by the *linguistic usage*.

We can conclude from this that if we wish to describe a language, the worst conceivable procedure will be the one that might appear, from a superficial and external point of view, to be the most natural one and the only one possible—that of beginning with an enumeration of the signs that are used in the language. Obviously, if one wishes to learn a language it is not enough to know the linguistic structure—one must also know the linguistic usage. But the usage presupposes the structure, so one's labors are considerably shortened if one begins by studying the structure. The number of expression elements in a language is quite limited: twenty-odd would be common; more than fifty would be very rare. The number of syllables in a language can often be written with four digits. The number of signs, on the other hand, can go into the tens of thousands and is, in fact, by the nature of language, unlimited. A list of the signs of a language—a dictionary—is always necessarily incomplete, if only because new signs are being formed while the dictionary is being compiled and many more have been formed before the dictionary finds its last user. And yet the language in which these new signs are formed is still the same as when the dictionary was begun. A language remains the same as long as the linguistic structure is the same, and one and the same language can be subjected to different linguistic usages and put to different applications. English continues to be English even if new words are introduced into it, provided only that the words are formed according to the same rules for constructing syllables and are composed of the same elements as before.

Thus it is the linguistic structure, and that alone, that determines the identity and constancy of a language. As long as we have the same linguistic structure, we can say meaningfully that we have the same language. Without this criterion we should have to be content with observing that a language is forever changing and that each morning we wake up to a different language from the one we had the day before. Each morning we find in the newspaper some sign or other that is new in English, or at any rate new to us. Without this criterion, moreover, we should never be justified in saying that we knew a language: nobody knows and understands all the signs that have been used in English or all the signs that are being used daily by specialists in this or that field, or by people of certain regions or of certain milieus.

Linguistic structure not only determines the identity of a language; it is also what essentially determines the difference between languages. A person who knows only one language or a few languages of approximately the same structure will be inclined to believe that the rules for combining elements have, so to speak, a natural inevitability. And if he is told that some combination or other is not permitted in English, he will perhaps be inclined to think that this is simply because the combination cannot come from human lips. Actually, it is only his own habits of pronunciation that are involved. With respect to combinations of sounds, there is very little that is impossible. Our speech organs are natural Jacks-of-all-trades. We have simply got them into the habit of being able to produce only a very few of the movements that they could produce if we had trained them differently, i.e. for purposes other than those laid down by our native language. *vlk* and *krk* are impossible words in English, but perfectly good words in Czech (where they mean 'wolf' and 'neck' respectively); *lgat'* and *rvat'* would be unthinkable as English words, but are all right in Russian (with the meanings 'to lie' and 'to tear'); Georgian (a language spoken in the Caucasus) can furnish words that a native speaker of English, because of his speech habits, would believe to be physically impossible—words like *vhsdšam* 'I eat', *mtha* 'hill', *mkbenare* 'biting', *dsqali* 'water'. A word like *squelch,* on the other hand, would cause a Finn or a Frenchman insuperable difficulties, if only because Finnish permits no consonant clusters at the beginning of a syllable and French no consonant clusters at the end.

The relationship between elements and signs that we have been discussing here is the real secret of the whole marvelously practical mechanism of language—indeed, one might be tempted to say, the touch of genius in the construction of language. It is always possible to form new signs simply by putting together in a new way the same familiar elements according to the same familiar rules, and both the elements and the rules are few and quickly learned. Given once and for all a handful of elements together with their rules of combination, we have an inexhaustible number of possible combinations and hence of signs. The system of elements is closed, once and for all, but the system of signs is productive; the elements constitute a closed set, but the signs an open one; within any one language the number of the elements is unalterable, but the number of signs can be augmented according to the needs and pleasure of the society or of the individual (e.g. the poet or the technical specialist) and can also be diminished as certain words drop out of use and are discarded because they are superfluous or unwanted. Being so fluid, the sign system is not merely applicable to certain situations but adaptable, without restriction, to new situations of any kind. This is why no language is bound to any particular conceptual sphere, to any particular milieu, or to any particular culture. Experts on American Indian languages have rightly emphasized that those languages would be just as well qualified as any other to express Western European culture even though, so long as they serve Indian culture, they have not yet formed signs for many of our concepts, such as those of technical and scientific origin. Let the need arise, and they would be able to form such signs in a completely suitable way. Every language

has, in addition to signs already in use, a practically inexhaustible reserve of unused possible signs.

Consequently, one can imagine a language used in many
different ways. The same linguistic structure can be matched
with quite different linguistic usages. One could take the whole
English dictionary and replace all the words it contains with
other, newly formed words that it does not contain and still
preserve the English linguistic structure intact, simply by using
the same elements, and only those, and combining them in
syllables according to the same rules.

But while many different linguistic usages can thus be
matched to one and the same linguistic structure, the converse
is not true. Only one linguistic structure can be matched with a
given linguistic usage. In the function between linguistic structure and linguistic usage, the structure is a *constant* and the
usage a *variable*. This is what makes it reasonable to say that it
is the structure and not the usage that determines the identity
of a language and defines one language as opposed to another.

The linguistic structure, then, fixes the number of elements
and the way in which each of these elements can be combined
with others. That is all. All other phenomena observed in language may vary in relation to this, and they therefore constitute
usage. Examples are the formation of signs and the utilization
of possible signs, but other phenomena as well are variables in
relation to the linguistic structure and therefore also belong to
the linguistic usage. The representation of the elements (cf. p.
13) is not fixed by the linguistic structure and may vary arbitrarily with respect to it. The elements in a linguistic structure
may be represented in any way whatsoever, provided only that
the elements required by the structure are kept distinct. The
elements may, for example, be represented graphically, with
each element having its own letter. So long as the letters are
distinct from one another, they may have any shape desired.
We are free to choose and vary their form, color, etc. while still
preserving the linguistic structure. We could represent the

same linguistic structure with a freshly invented writing system or with a code of special conventional signs, and the language would still remain the same. Thus it is possible to represent the English expression elements in non-Latin alphabets or in Morse code and still have perfectly good English. The elements can also be represented phonetically, each element by its own sound, no matter what, so long as it is sufficiently distinct from the others. (The human ear can be trained to hear very fine nuances, so what was said above about the organs of speech applies here: the ear, too, is a Jack-of-all-trades, but the special training it has had in hearing the nuances that play a role in the native language reduces its ability to hear the nuances that play a role in other languages, so that a person will often be inclined to declare it physically impossible to perceive the distinctions utilized in a language not his own.) It is equally immaterial how the sounds are produced—whether by phonograph, sound film, signal-whistle, or human mouth and throat. The elements of the linguistic structure can equally well be represented by other means, such as flags of different designs and colors. This is the way in which ships all over the world communicate with one another in English or any other language, using an international signaling system. Individual navies have such flag codes of their own, by means of which they communicate in their native languages. The manual alphabet of deaf mutes is another special way of representing the expression elements of a language. We could go on citing such examples, and to the extent of our inventiveness, we could construct ever new means for executing one and the same linguistic structure, new means for speaking one and the same language.

The elements of the linguistic structure call to mind the entities used in algebra—like $a$, $b$, $c$, $x$, $y$, $z$—for which we can substitute different numerals in arithmetic and different numbers, with their different names, in practical reckoning. So long as we abide by the expressed conditions, we can represent the algebraic entities as we will.

To use a comparison that may perhaps be carried further, we can say that a language is organized like a game—like chess or like a card game, for example. The elements are the pieces or the cards. Different languages, like different games, have rules that differ in whole or in part. These rules state how a given element, whether piece or card, may be used and how it may not. To some extent, they restrict the possibilities of combination, but the number of permitted combinations or sign formations, in a language as in chess, is still enormous. The totality of the rules, stating how many pieces there are in a game and how each piece may be combined with others, can be called the structure of the game; and it differs from the usage of the game just as the linguistic structure differs from the linguistic usage. An account of the usage of the game would have to include information not only about the way one is *permitted* to act (this is the structure of the game), but also how people are accustomed to acting in given situations or have in fact acted up to now (this is the usage of the game)—in other words, what combinations have time-honored status under given conditions. In the same way an account of the linguistic usage would have to include information about the customary use of signs at a definite point in time in a definite milieu under given conditions. An account of the usage of the game would also have to include information about the material of which the pieces are usually made, or have been made, or are most appropriately made, and would have to tell us how each piece or kind of piece usually looks or has looked (the knight in chess looks like a horse's head, and so on)—and in just the same way, an account of the linguistic usage would also have to include a description of the material (graphic, phonetic, and so on) of which the elements are made, and would have to tell us in detail how the individual graphs, sounds, etc., are constituted. Every usage of a game presupposes the structure of the game, but not conversely. And many different game usages can be matched to one and the same game structure. The structure of a game remains the same, whatever use is made of its rules. This is precisely the reason why the same game structure can be used over and over again for new combinations—new games—just as the same linguistic structure can be used over and over again to form new signs. And the structure of the game remains the same, even if the pieces are made of a different material or given a different shape. In this respect the structure of the game allows complete freedom, with the one restriction that pieces differing in their rules of combination must be sufficiently distinguishable. In this connexion, it may be recalled that one can play chess by telegraph, without using pieces at all but representing the elements of the game by signs in Morse code.

In using a language, people will easily come to associate with it, more or less consciously, certain notions of very different kinds. These notions may also be counted as part of the linguistic usage; in any event, they clearly do not belong to the linguistic structure. As a rule, they are notions directly associated in one way or another with the external shapes of the element-representatives—with the shapes of sounds, for example, or of letters. It will be felt that some are beautiful and others ugly, or that some are similar and others not, or that some resemble things outside language while others do not. An example of this last situation is what is customarily called *sound-symbolism*. Because words like *little, bit, kid,* or *pin* include an element phonetically represented in the linguistic usage by a certain sound (written *i*), and because in one way or another their content of meaning suggests the notion of smallness, the definite impression may be formed that there is some vague connexion between that sound and the notion of something small. It must be noted at once that these questions of similarity or dissimilarity between sounds, or between letters, or between sounds or letters on the one hand and things outside language on the other, are purely subjective, depending entirely on the point of view from which the comparison is made. Two things are never similar in every respect, but only in some respect;

and given sufficient ingenuity we can always find some respect in which two things are similar, however different they may be. On my desk is an object which, in respect of shape, resembles a dog; in respect of material, it most resembles a bunch of pipe cleaners; in respect of color, it resembles dirty snow; and so on. In the same way, with enough imagination, any two speech sounds or any two sign-meanings can be found to resemble each other.

All these notions attached to the external shapes of the elem nt-representatives may, of course, also be attached to their usual combinations as permitted by the linguistic structure—to signs, for example, combinations of signs, turns of speech, and so on. And many of these notions, because of their particularly close connexion with the material of language or because the users of a language at a given point in time and in a given milieu are for some reason or other so disposed, become collective notions which most members of a linguistic community hold more or less clearly—or can easily be led to believe that they hold. We call the totality of all such notions a *feeling for a language*, or *Sprachgefühl*. Obviously, this is a psychological phenomenon, the study of which requires the collaboration of psychologists and linguists; as yet, it is for the most part unexplored territory.

# *Sign Formation*

Since the linguistic community is free to introduce new signs and discard old ones at will, it is obvious that the Sprachgefühl, especially in so far as it is collective, will be a decisive factor in sign formation. The counter-examples to the element-functions, which we are now about to discuss, are due precisely to the fact that signs can be transformed or created on the basis of a given Sprachgefühl. Since, as we have seen, such feeling for a language is unexplored territory and, by its very nature, quite intangible, we might seem to be in a poor position to make any precise delimitation of these counter-examples. If we can nevertheless do so, it is because we can be satisfied, to a large extent, with substituting for that feeling the objective factors (phonetic, linguistic, etc.) to which it is attached.

We shall now review the most important kinds of sign formation and show how they produce counter-examples to the element-functions.

## I. FUNCTIONAL TRANSFORMATION OF SIGNS

### I 1. Action of elements

Within a chain of elements ( a word, for example), one element may cause the appearance at another place in the same chain of a different element from the one expected. For example, corresponding to the preposition that appears as Goth. *fair-*, Ir. *air-*, Gr. *pér*, *péri*, *perí*, Lith. *per-*, OCS *prě-*, and OI *pári* (having such meanings as 'about, through, for' in the different languages), the Indo-European element-functions would lead us to expect Lat. *per*, with *r* according to the function given on pp. 16–17. And indeed, the word actually is *per* in Latin. Now this word can be compounded with the word *ager* 'field, territory, territory country' to form the verb *per-agrāre* 'to through-country', i.e. 'travel through, wander through' and the adverb *per-egrī, per-egrē* 'abroad' (with *e* in place of *a* under conditions that we can ignore for the moment), from which is derived *per-egrīnus* 'foreigner, stranger'. All this is in agreement with the element-functions. But the word may also appear in Latin as *pelegrīnus*, a form that we know from inscriptions. And the various Romance forms of the same word (It. *pellegrino*, Sp. *pelegrino*, Fr. *pélerin*) presuppose the Vulgar Latin formula *\*pelegrinu*. This must also be the Latin form that was carried over into Germanic, as in OHG *piligrîm*, Dan. *pil(e)grim*, and Eng. *pilgrim*. But this form with *l* is not in agreement with the element-functions. It is due to the action of one element in the word, the *r* in the syllable -*grī*-, which has caused the unexpected appearance of *l* in place of the *r* in the syllable -*re*-.

The reason for this counter-example is obviously that the same element, *r*, would have appeared in two places in the word. The counter-example has a psychological cause, namely the fact that under certain conditions it is more difficult to maintain two elements of the same kind than two different ones. Since this is a psychological matter, we can never predict whether it will or will not occur. But it has proved to be possible to establish general laws by which we can predict (1) what particular structure characterizes the words that may be replaced by such transformations, so that we can remove them from consideration when studying the element-functions, and (2) which element in a word of given structure will be affected by the change if the change takes place. Before demonstrating this, we can state in general that the replacing element introduced when a sign is so transformed will always be an element already admitted by the linguistic structure concerned. The transformation never involves an increase or a diminution in the inventory of elements in the language, and it takes place in agreement with the rules for sign formation that can be deduced from the rules of the linguistic structure governing the use of the elements. Within these limits, however, there is a certain freedom with respect to the *choice* of the replacing element (provided the linguistic structure allows a choice between two or more possibilities at the given place in the syllable). The speakers choose the element that seems to them, on the basis of their feeling for the language, to lie nearest to the displaced element. It is always possible, however, to point out objective physical (most often, physiological) reasons why one sound will strike speakers of the language as being especially close to another sound, so that, given a general knowledge of the language's phonetic system, we can predict with a fair amount of certainty (in many instances, with complete certainty) which element will be chosen as replacement. If we make such a preliminary calculation about *r* on the basis of a phonetic analysis of the Latin sound system (which we shall not undertake here), we arrive at the unambiguous conclusion that the only possible replacement is *l*.

As to which element in a word of given structure will be affected by the change, if the change occurs, three factors will be decisive:

1. whether the elements involved enter into a stressed or unstressed syllable;

2. whether they are found in the *initial, central,* or *final field* of the syllable (in a syllable like *stand, s* and *t* are in the initial field, *a* is in the central field, and *n* and *d* are in the final field; in a syllable like *at,* the initial field is lacking, *a* is in the central field, and *t* is in the final; in a syllable like *ma, m* is in the initial field, *a* is in the central field, and the final field is lacking; in the syllable *a,* both initial and final fields are lacking);

3. whether they are found *alone* in the field (like *t* in *at,* or *m* in *ma,* or *t* and *p* in *tap*) or enter into a group (like *s* and *t,* or *n* and *d,* in *stand*), and whether they are *covered* or *uncovered* (a covered

element is an element in initial field following immediately an element in final field of the preceding syllable: the *t* in *pantry* is covered, the *t* in *poetry* is not).

With the help of these definitions we can fully establish general laws stating which element in a word may be subjected to the action of another element. In what follows, we shall examine only a few examples of such general laws.

## I 1 a. *Dissimilation*

In dissimilation, speakers avoid repeating the same physiological movements in the representation of two elements. The word *pelegrīnus* is an example: replacement of *r* by *l* eliminates repetition of the tongue movement needed to pronounce *r*. Another example is Lat. *tenebrae* 'darkness', corresponding to OI *támisrā*. From the element-functions (cf. p. 15) we should expect a Latin *m* in correspondence to Old Indic *m*. The *n* that we find in Latin has been introduced by dissimilation, eliminating the repetition of lip movements used in the pronunciation of both *m* and *b*. From this last example we see that dissimilation may occur even if two elements are not completely identical, just so long as they have in common some characteristic movement of the organs of speech. In most cases of dissimilation, however, there is complete identity, so that most of the vocabulary that may be affected by dissimilation, and that must therefore be removed from consideration when we are studying the element-functions, consists of words in which the same element appears twice, with one or more elements in between.

The fact that in *peregrīnus* it is the first, and not the second, *r* that may be affected by dissimilation is due to the general law that an element in a group in a stressed syllable dissimilates an element standing alone between two vowels—never the other way round. Thus it is inconceivable that a form *peregrīnus* would arise from dissimilation; if *peregrīnus* is subjected to dissimilation, *pelegrīnus* is the only possible result. By virtue of the same general law, *cérébral* 'cerebral' is dissimilated in popular French to *célébral*, *contrario* 'contrary' in Galician (spoken in northwestern Spain) to *contralio*, *imperatrīce(m)* 'empress' in Portuguese to *empānatriz*, and so on.

The fact that in a case like *temebrae* it is the *m* and not the *b* that may be (and in this example actually was) affected by dissimilation is due to the general law that, of two elements having the same definition according to the criteria on pp. 47–48, it is always the first, and never the second, that is dissimilated. In *temebrae*, *m* and *b* have the same definition in this respect: both are in unstressed syllable (the stress is on the first syllable of the word), both are in the initial field of their syllable, and both are uncovered. The syllable with *m* comes before the syllable with *b*, so it is the *m* that must give way. By virtue of the same law, Fr. *militaire* is dissimilated in popular speech in *mélitaire*: both *i*'s are in unstressed syllable and in the central field—hence the first *i* is dissimilated, not the second.

If Fr. *barbier*, derived from *barbe* 'beard', can appear in German as *Balbier* and in Danish as *balbér*, but not the other way round as *barbiel*, *barbél*, this is due to the general law that an element in the final field of the stressed syllable dissimilates an element in the final field of the unstressed syllable, and not the other way round. This is why we also find Lat. *arbor* 'tree', Fr. *arbre*, appearing in Spanish as *árbol*, and Lat. *marmor* 'marble' appearing in Spanish as *mármol* and in German and older Danish as *Marmel*.

Another such general law states that a covered element dissimilates an uncovered one, never vice versa. This explains the change of the Latin numeral *quīnque* 'five' to *cinque*, which is the basis for Fr. *cinq*, It. *cinque*, etc. The Italian word *tartufolo* was carried over into German as *Tartuffel*, but in accordance with this general law of dissimilation, was changed in both German and Danish to *Kartoffel* 'potato'. Dissimilations like *quince* or *tarkoffel* would be inconceivable.

## I 1 b. *Metathesis*

Metathesis (in the restricted sense in which we shall use the word here) is a transfer of an element from one syllable to another. It is found in two forms:

1. Transfer of one element. This always consists in the transfer of an element in a group from an unstressed to a stressed syllable—never otherwise. By this form of metathesis Italian has acquired the word *coccodrillo* in place of Lat. *crocodilus*. The form with metathesis evidently existed in Late Latin and was carried over into Middle High German, where it is *kokodrille*.

2. Interchange of two or more elements. In the simplest and most frequent cases, two elements in neighboring syllables are interchanged. This always takes place in such a way that elements not appearing in the order of expiration are transposed so that they do. (Order of expiration is the order of movements of speech organs from the interior to the exterior—from throat to lips.) We have discussed above (p. 19) the Latin word *specere*, a word also known from Old Indic, where it appears as *spáśati*. These forms establish the Indo-European formula for the root as *$spek_1$-. But in Greek the word meaning 'to look, view, examine' is *sképtesthai* (from which are derived the well-known word *sképsis* 'examination, speculation' and *skeptikós* 'one who speculates or reflects', carried over into Eng. *skeptic*). This is due to a metathesis by which the *p-k* sequence has been changed to *k-p* because the *k*-sound is formed farther back in the mouth than the *p*-sound: the *p*-sound is a labial stop, while the *k*-sound is produced by an occlusion between the tongue and the palate.

Other kinds of metathesis are governed by other laws, which we shall not discuss here.

## I 1 c. *Haplology*

This term refers to the omission of a syllable on account of its similarity (most often an identity) to a neighboring syllable: *tragicomic* for *tragico-comic*, *mineralogy* for *mineralo-logy*.

Almost all the general laws that we know governing the action of elements were discovered by the French scholar Maurice Grammont. Some of these laws may well need closer scrutiny, but there is no doubt that general laws can be established. Apparent exceptions can be explained by the fact that a word will often have been subjected to several successive transformations, so that a given form is not always to be explained merely by the mechanical application of some single law. Moreover, Grammont foresaw the possibility that the blind action of a law may lead to results conflicting with the linguistic structure by producing an inadmissible type of syllable. In such a case, he calculated that the tendency to dissimilation or metathesis, if sufficiently strong, will have its effect under a set of laws opposed to those discussed above; but even then, there will be no suspension of law, since such cases can be clearly circumscribed and defined.

## I 2. Analogical formation

By analogical formation we mean an action of signs. When there is a paradigm of signs (of words, for example), one member of the paradigm may cause the appearance at another place in the paradigm of a different sign from the one expected. There are three main types of analogical formation.

### I 2 a. *Leveling*

Leveling occurs when two members in a paradigm are brought closer together in form. In the nominative singular, the second personal pronoun of Indo-European appears as both *tu* and *tū*, as attested by Goth. *þu*, Ir. *tú*, Lat. *tū*, Lith. *tù*, OCS *ty*, etc. The other cases are formed on a stem consisting of *t* or *tu̯* followed by a vowel. In the accusative this vowel is *e* or *ē*, so that we start with the forms *te* or *tē*—found, for example, in Lat. *tē* and ON *þi-k* (the Gmc. *-k* corresponds to Gr. *-ge*, a particle that can be added to pronouns; cf. Goth. *mi-k*, p. 14)— and the forms *tu̯e* or *tu̯ē*—found at the base of such forms as Hitt. *twel* 'thee, thine', *twetaz* 'of thee, from thee' or OI *tvam* 'thou'. In Greek, some dialects have the accusative form *te*—as in Doric *té*—and others have *tu̯e*—as in Attic-Ionic *sé* (where *s-* = IE *tu̯-*); other cases of the same word are formed on *t-* and *tu-* with the same dialectal distribution (dative: Doric *toí*, Attic-Ionic *soí*; cf. OI *tve*). All this is in accord with the element-functions, and our paradigms are what we should expect:

|  | ON | Lat. | Dor. |
|---|---|---|---|
| Nominative | *þú* | *tū* | *tú* |
| Accusative | *þi-k* | *tē* | *té* |

In Gothic, however, the accusative is not *þi-k*, as it is in Old Norse and as we should expect from Indo-European *te-ge*, but *þu-k*. A leveling has taken place, bringing the two members of the paradigm closer together in form and thereby producing a counter-example to the element-functions: a Gmc. *u* cannot be an IE *e* (or *ē*). In Hittite, we find something even stranger: the nominative is *zik* (= IE *te-ge*) and the accusative *tuk* (= IE *tu-ge*). This paradigm is the result of two contradictory levelings, each striving to bring the two members of the paradigm closer together in form, which paradoxically enough have led to a compromise no better than the point of departure. Greek also shows a leveling in this paradigm, but in another way: the Attic-Ionic nominative is not *tú*, like the Doric, but *sú*, showing analogical influence from those cases in which the word begins with *s-* (= IE *tu̯*).

Other instances of levelings that produce counter-examples to the element-functions can be found in the numerals. Indo-European 'four' and 'five' are *$k_3$etu̯ōres* (cf. Lat. *quattuor*, Lith. *keturì*, OI *catvā́raḥ*) and *$pénk_3e$* (cf. Lith. *penkì*, OI *páñca*). They begin with two quite different consonants, to which the word-initial element-functions will assign quite different correspondences in Germanic. IE *$k_3$-* appears in Germanic as *hw-*, as shown in the interrogative pronoun: Goth. *hwas*, genitive

*hwis*; Lat. *quis*, feminine *quae*; Lith. *kàs*; OI *kaḥ*, etc. IE *$p$-
appears in Germanic as *f-*, as we know from *father* and similar
examples. Nevertheless, not only the numeral *five*, but also the
numeral *four* begins with an *f-* in Germanic: Goth. *fidwor* 'four',
*fimf* 'five'. (The final *f* in *fimf* corresponding to IE *$k_3$ is in accordance with an element-function: *$k_3$ has Germanic correspondence *f* if there is a preceding *$p$ or *$u$ in the same word—cf.
Goth. *wulfs* 'wolf', Lith. *vìlkas*, OCS *vlьkъ*, OI *vṛkaḥ*, IE *$ulk_3os$.
We may also note that the first *qu* in Lat. *quīnque* corresponding
to IE *$p$ is in accordance with an element-function: *$p$ has
Latin correspondence *qu* or *c*, depending on the following vowel,
if there is a following *$k_3$ in the same word—cf. *coquere* 'to
cook', OCS *pekǫ*, OI *pácati*.) The reason for *f-* in Goth. *fidwor*,
Eng. *four*, instead of the expected Goth. *hw-*, Eng. *wh-*, is an
analogical leveling that has brought two members of the paradigm of numerals closer together in form.

In general, levelings are common in the paradigm of numerals.
The numeral *nine* begins with *$n$- (cf., for example, Lat. *novem*,
OI *náva*), while the numeral *ten* begins with *$d$- (see p. 19), but
in the Baltic and Slavic languages both numerals begin with
*$d$-' (Lith. *devynì*, *dẽšimt*, OCS *devętъ*, *desętъ*): the *$d$- in 'nine'
has been introduced by leveling. According to the element-
functions, we should expect Lat. *quīnque* (with the dissimilation
discussed on p. 49) to end in *-e* in Spanish. In fact, it ends in
*-o* (*cinco*), under the analogical influence of *cuatro* 'four'. Similarly, Italian has final *-i* in *dieci* 'ten' (Lat. *decem*) by leveling
with *venti* 'twenty' (Lat. *uīgintī*).

Paradigms like those we have been considering—the case
paradigm of a pronoun and the paradigm of numerals—are
given in the linguistic structure itself and constitute absolutely
closed series with a limited number of members. (Even though
the numbers constitute an infinite series, the series of number
*words* is finite and, indeed, always fairly short, with most numbers being designated by a combination of two or more words.)

But in linguistic usage we are faced with many paradigms having an unlimited number of members, since, as we have seen, the sign system is not closed, but productive. Here, where Sprachgefühl will be uncertain in its arbitrary selection of the paradigm to which a given sign shall be allotted, it will play fast and free, haphazardly, and on the basis of very loose associations. If the Indo-European word for 'eye' begins with *o- (cf., for example, Lat. *oculus*, OCS *oko*) and the Indo-European word for 'ear' begins with *au̯- (cf. Lat. *auris*, Lith. *ausìs*), while both words begin with *au̯ in Germanic (Goth. *augo, auso*, Dan. *øje, øre*), the state of affairs in Germanic will be due to a leveling, caused by the fact that linguistic feeling readily tends to locate the two words in the same paradigm. Ger. *Sauerkraut* has been taken over into French as *choucroute* because Sprachgefühl has located it in the same paradigm as *chou* 'cabbage' on the basis of similarity in meaning and has thus produced a leveling that brings the two members of the paradigm closer together in form. In the same way, Fr. *mousqueton* 'carbine', a derivative of *mousquet* 'musket', was carried over into German in the form *Muskedonner* under the influence of *Donner* 'thunder', and into Norwegian and Swedish in the form *muskedunder* under the influence of the word *dunder* 'din, uproar'. This kind of leveling, which depends on loose associations in the Sprachgefühl and arbitrary linkage of two signs in a single paradigm, is called *popular etymology*.

Levelings are the only analogical formations that commonly produce true counter-examples to the element-functions. For this reason, we shall consider only very briefly the two other kinds of analogical formation.

## I 2 b. *Contamination*

By contamination is meant the blending of two members of a paradigm into one, as *irrespective* and *regardless* into *irregardless*, or *snort* and *chuckle* into Lewis Carroll's *chortle*, or *breakfast* and *lunch* into *brunch*.

## I 2 c. *Proportional formation*

In proportional formation a sign is transferred to a different paradigm from the one to which it previously belonged. The strong and weak verbs of English constitute two different paradigms, but many formerly strong verbs have been transferred by proportional formation to the weak paradigm, producing new forms like *helped* for older *holp*. The different declensions and grammatical genders likewise constitute different paradigms. In German, the word *Nacht* 'night' belongs to a paradigm consisting of feminine nouns that take umlaut in the plural (*Nächte*), while *Tag* 'day' belongs to a paradigm consisting of masculine nouns that have "strong" declension (genitive *Tags*) and do not take umlaut in the plural (*Tage*). The genitive of *Nacht* in the definite form is *der Nacht*, but still 'at night' can be *des Nachts*, just as 'in the daytime' is *des Tages*: a proportional formation has brought *Nacht* into the same paradigm as *Tag*.

We call these formations proportional because they presuppose the construction of a proportion or equation of the type $a:b = c:x$, with solution $x = b'$; for example, *hinder*:*hindered* = *help*:$x$, therefore $x = helped$. Contamination, on the other hand, follows the formula $a \times b = c$; thus, *breakfast* $\times$ *lunch* = *brunch*.

Since the sign system is subject to the arbitrariness of linguistic usage, and since Sprachgefühl is unpredictable, it is clear that general laws cannot be established in this area as they can for the action of elements. But perhaps this is only because the linguistic content has not yet been adequately analyzed from a psychological point of view. If the actions of elements have been so thoroughly explored, it is precisely because we are able to analyze the sounds of language and because we know something about the psychology of sound. Perhaps in the future we shall have more solid bases than at present for the study of analogical formations. Meanwhile, our experience with the genetic study of an enormous amount of linguistic material has shown that analogical formations in no way prevent us from getting to know the element-functions and, in general, cause no practical difficulties in our investigations. We have only to be aware of the fact that the principle of analogical formation provides a reason for setting aside certain counter-examples with which we may have to deal.

## I 3. Abbreviation of signs

A sign may undergo abbreviation when transferred in certain ways to a different category from the one to which it previously belonged. The most important instances are the following:

1. A compound word becomes simple. Thus, compounds originally meaning 'loaf-ward' and, probably, 'loaf-kneader' became simplified in English to result in present-day *lord* and *lady*.

2. A derivative word becomes a non-derivative. Thus, Ger. *fressen* 'to eat (of animals), to cram' has replaced *ver-essen* (Goth. *fra-itan*), and Ger. *gleich* 'equal, like' has ·replaced *ge-leich* (Goth. *ga-leiks*; cf. also, without the derivational prefix, Dan. *lig*, Eng. *like*, and Lith. *lýgus* 'straight, smooth, like').

3. A sign is transferred to another grammatical category and shortened in the process. Thus, a substantive transmuted into a preposition is often abbreviated. Lat. *casa* 'hut' (It. *casa* 'house') appears in Old French as *chiese*, in accordance with the element-functions involved. But the phrase *in casa* followed by a genitive, meaning 'in so-and-so's house', was transferred to the category of prepositions and took on the meaning 'at (so-and-so's)'. In consequence, the final vowel dropped, and the result was OF *en chies*, Modern Fr. *chez* (without *en*). The corresponding Danish preposition *hos* bears the same relation to the noun *hus* 'house'; cf. also Dan. *til*, Eng. *till*, and Ger. *Ziel* 'goal, target, term'.

Another instance of the same kind is the transfer of a verb to the category of auxiliary verbs. A Latin *b* between two vowels appears as *v* in French: Lat. *faba* 'bean', Fr. *fève*; Lat. *dēbēre* 'owe, ought', Fr. *devoir*; Lat. *habēre* 'have', Fr. *avoir*. But corresponding to Lat. *habeō* 'I have' we find Fr. *ai*, with zero instead of the expected *v*. The reason is that the verb has become an auxiliary and has consequently been abbreviated. We should, then, really expect to find *j'ai* used as an auxiliary (as in *j'ai mangé* 'I have eaten') and another form, containing *v*, used as a full verb. The fact that we find *j'ai* in this function also (*j'ai un ami* 'I have a friend') is due to a generalizing analogical formation.

The categories we have considered so far—compound, derivative, substantive and preposition, full verb and auxiliary verb—are given in the linguistic structure itself. But categories may also be established by the linguistic usage. Such category formation, however, is very easily delimited: a category may be established consisting of signs that are in especially frequent use and are consequently abbreviated.

4. A sign is abbreviated because of frequent use. We can begin by discussing some borderline cases which may also involve transfer to a category given in the linguistic structure. In Latin, the imperative of consonant-stem (third-conjugation) verbs ends in *-e* (= IE *-e*): *scrīb-e* 'write!' from the verb *scrībere*. But the five verbs *dīcere* 'say', *dūcere* 'lead', *facere* 'do', *ferre* 'carry', and *emere* 'buy' have imperative forms *dīc*, *dūc*, *fac*, *fer*, and *em*, without *-e*. (The form *em* has the special meaning 'there! see!' while 'buy!' is *em-e*. The verb is found with the meaning 'take' in other Indo-European languages, e.g. Lith. *im̃ti*, OCS *ęti*.) Here we might say that these imperatives have been transferred to the category of interjections, which is surely to be found in the linguistic structure. We find the same situation when an answer-word like *yes* or *no* appears, as it often does, in a form conflicting with the element-functions. Answer-words also constitute a category, which is defined by its special relation to the environments and which is therefore also to be found in the

linguistic structure. Here also belong forms of address, which we often find quite radically abbreviated: Fr. *monsieur* is pronounced *m'sieu*, Eng. *madam* collapses to *mam* or merely *m*, especially when combined with an answer-word (*yes'm*). In the same way, Russ. *gosudár'*, first shortened to *súdar'*, was further reduced to *s* alone when combined with an answer-word (*da-s* 'yes, sir'). In this way doublets often arise, one of which retains its full lexical meaning while the other has been reduced to a more or less empty formula of politeness. Words meaning 'you' also frequently turn out to be abbreviations of longer complexes: Sp. *Usted* is a compression of *Vuestra merced* 'Your Grace', and Lith. *Támsta* of *tàvo mýlista* 'Thy Grace'.

But even if there is a clear connexion here with categories anchored in the linguistic structure, we still must recognize in the linguistic usage the existence of a category of signs that are used with special frequency and therefore abbreviated. Thus, not only is *automobile vehicle*, Fr. *voiture automobile*, abbreviated to *automobile*, but the latter is further curtailed—in French, English, German, and several other languages, to *auto*, and in Danish to *bil*. In the same way, *airplane* is shortened to *plane*, and Dan. *flyvemaskine* 'flying machine' to *fly*. Abbreviations of this sort are especially common in professional jargons, because certain signs are used with high frequency by professional people in a particular field (though they may be strange or completely unknown to others). English students' vocabulary provides examples like *lab* (also found in German and Danish) for *laboratory*, *exam* for *examination*, *prep* for *preparation*, and *prof* for *professor*. As a rule, in these cases, too, the shorter form coexists with the longer and has no different meaning; it is not really a new sign, but a sign-variant, quite on a line with abbreviations in the written language. Moreover, such formations, unlike many others, are produced quite consciously, by a voluntary interference in the language. Some linguistic communities are more inclined to introduce them than others, and this often depends on the general structure of signs in the given language. English, which already has so many monosyllabic words that it seems natural to introduce more, favors this kind of abbreviation. Danish is considerably more conservative in this respect, a fact undoubtedly connected with the structure of the language, according to which abbreviation often involves a change in pronunciation. Despite its usefulness, *fly* is a bit inconvenient as an abbreviation of *flyvemaskine* because it cannot be pronounced completely like the first syllable of the longer word: Danish linguistic structure requires the addition of a glottal catch to the monosyllable *fly* that the unabbreviated word does not contain. Norwegian and Swedish, which do not have this difficulty, adopt such abbreviations much more easily.

In recent times, as is well known, German, Russian, and English have created a large number of abbreviation-names like *CDU* for *Christliche Demokratische Union, DDP* for *Deutsche Demokratische Partei, Komintérn* for *Kommunistíčeskij Internacionál, Komsomól* for *Kommunistíčeskij Sojúz Molodëži, UN* for *United Nations.* In Danish, abbreviations composed of initial syllables of words are not common (although we do find, in spoken as well as written Danish, such abbreviations of academic degrees as *stud. mag., mag. art.,* etc.). Danish prefers abbreviations composed of initial letters—which are also common in German and Russian. Where these produce possible syllables, some languages have a tendency to pronounce them so—as, for example, *URSS* may be pronounced in French.

## II. INTRODUCTION OF
## NEW SIGNS

### II 1. Borrowings

"Borrowing" (an established, but somewhat misleading term) means the transfer of a sign from one language to another. Most frequently, words or stems of words are so transferred, but other kinds of signs may also be borrowed, like the English prefix *inter-*, which comes from Latin but which can be added to genuine English words. Borrowed words are called *loan words*. Loan words whose external forms produce an alien or incongruous effect—by reason, say, of an unusual syllable-onset (*tsetse*) or special type of accentuation—are also called *foreign words*. What is characteristic of foreign words is that they do not follow the laws of the native linguistic structure, but of some foreign structure. They are like minorities living under their own special laws. Consequently, they are often subject to transformation by unlearned speakers following their native Sprachgefühl, or to popular etymology (*very coarse veins* for *varicose veins*). As for loan words that are not foreign words, the man in the street has no suspicion of their origin and will be astounded when told that words like *skirt* (from Scandinavian), *street* (from Latin), or *chair* (from Old French) are loan words.

When a word has been borrowed from a known source, it is, of course, easy enough to demonstrate its identity, but the element-functions will not ordinarily hold. We have already had occasion to refer to words that have been carried over in this way from one language to another: Greek and Latin borrowings in Germanic, like *fraternize* (p. 11), *paternity* (p. 13), *pecuniary* (p. 18), *inspect* (p. 19), *pilgrim* (p. 46), *crocodile* (p. 50), *skeptic* (p. 50), and others; French borrowings in Germanic, like *barber* (p. 49) and *Muskedonner* (p. 54); Italian borrowings in Germanic like *Kartoffel* (p. 49); German borrowings in French like *choucroute* (p. 54). We can see that while the element-functions have word-initial Gmc. *f-* corresponding to Lat. *p-* (*father, fee*), the Latin borrowings with initial *p-* appear in Germanic with *p-* (*paternity, pecuniary*). In this case, and in the vast majority of cases, there is an identity between the letter or sound in the lending and in the borrowing language. To this need only be added that loan words which do not continue to be foreign words are adapted not only to the native linguistic structure, but also to the native linguistic usage; such adaptation is normally the first step toward the assimilation of a loan word into the borrowing language. Thus, for example, we pronounce *psychology* without the *p* (adaptation to English linguistic structure) and a French loan word like *faux* (in *faux pas*) with the sounds we use in pronouncing English *foe* (adaptation to English linguistic usage).

There are, however, instances—although rather less frequent —when the loan word is transformed at the time of borrowing so as to accord in whole or, usually, only in part with the element-functions between the lending and the borrowing languages (provided, of course, they are genetically related). If this is to happen, the linguistic community must contain enough bilingual speakers whose Sprachgefühl makes them conscious of the regular element-functions between the two languages. Thus, there has been a consciousness in Denmark (undoubtedly influenced by the Low German borrowings in Danish) that Dan. *sk* corresponds to Ger. *sch* (pronounced [š]), as illustrated by such pairs as *skabe—schaffen*, *skade—schaden*, and *sko—Schuh*. Consequently, the French word *jus* 'juice', which is pronounced [žy] and was borrowed into German with the pronunciation [šy] by adaptation to German linguistic usage, appears in Danish, which has borrowed it from the German, as *sky* 'gravy'.

The speakers of a language, however, are rarely such competent linguists as to carry off a "fraud" like this successfully. Sprachgefühl will normally be concerned only with certain differences between languages that are particularly striking to the ear. In practice, then, it is almost always possible to detect from a word's external form whether it is a loan word. Indeed, the external form of the word is the linguist's only criterion. If a word can be shown to be connected with a word in another language but fails to conform to the element-functions that have been established on the basis of other examples and cannot be explained in any other way (by the action of elements, by analogical formation, or by the introduction of a new sign in some different fashion), it must be concluded that the word has been borrowed. Borrowing is thus an explanation that the linguist always has in reserve when other explanations fail. This does not mean, however, that we have created a convenient lumber room where we can dispose of obstinate cases by simply calling them "borrowings." As we have seen, borrowing is something quite precise and well defined, and the assumption of borrowing is logically compelling when other explanations are impossible. In all those instances where we can trace in detail the historical relationships and cultural influences that must be presupposed for the borrowing to have taken place, we can show that, whenever we find a word not genetically related to words in the genetically related languages and not explainable by the action of elements, by analogical formation, or by the introduction of a new sign in some different fashion, then the word *was*, indeed, introduced from outside at some determinable time and by some determinable route. There are, to be sure, many other cases where the external historical relationships and cultural currents are not so clearly known as to permit any such demonstration. But in such instances we generalize, just as science always does in like circumstances: from our knowledge of the fully elucidated cases we conclude hypothetically that the less well elucidated cases are of the same kind, provided there is nothing to contradict the assumption. In practice, then, the external shape of words is our only decisive criterion in establishing the fact of a borrowing, and by this purely linguistic means we are able to make inferences about prehistoric contacts of peoples and cultural currents that would otherwise remain completely unknown because no other sources of information are available.

If we leave out of account those cases—especially from more recent times—where the external historical circumstances are clearly known in full detail, so that the very introduction of the borrowing can be dated and investigated, there are no other general guidelines for the establishment of borrowing than internal, linguistic ones. In principle, there are no limits to what can be borrowed from one language into another. Often a sign will naturally be borrowed because it accompanies the thing it designates: an article of export carries its designation with it, as when Lat. *uīnum* 'wine' spread as a loan word over almost all the rest of Europe. But this is only a special case. A word is not borrowed merely because the thing it designates has no native designation. People borrow out of a desire to imitate, and borrowings are subject to all the caprices of fashion. People borrow because the foreign word is finer or more beautiful or more amusing or more interesting, and nobody can predict what people will consider fine, beautiful, amusing, or interesting. Bilingual populations may also, of course, introduce borrowings into a language simply because they have a hard time keeping the sign systems of the two languages apart. Examples of this can be found in all border regions. But this again is a special case. It is impossible before the event to say anything at all about what can and cannot be borrowed. The loan words in a language can rise to a formidable number. Albanian has been reported by some investigators to have only some six hundred words that are not borrowed, with all the rest coming from Latin, Romance languages, Slavic languages, Greek, and Turkish. Even a language like Greek, which is considered one of the purest Indo-European languages and which plays a greater role than any other in comparative Indo-European studies, contains only a relatively small number of words that can be genetically accounted for on the basis of Indo-European. Presumably, then, most Greek words are borrowings from other languages, chiefly, perhaps, from non–Indo-European languages. Just as we could observe above that some linguistic communities are more inclined than others to admit abbreviations of signs, we may say the same with respect to borrowings, without being able to offer any explanation for this difference. There are languages to which the many international words of Græco-Latin origin that abound in most modern European languages have a very hard time gaining admission, because the linguistic community prefers to use native lexical material to designate the things concerned. Thus, *university* in Icelandic is *háskóli* 'high school', in Finnish *yliopisto* 'institute of higher learning', and in Hungarian *egyetem*,

an artificial derivative from the numeral *egy* (pronounced [ɛď])
'one', in imitation of the Latin *ūniversitās*, a derivative from the
numeral *ūnus*; while other European languages use the international word that appears in English as *university*. Icelandic is
particularly famous (or, if preferred, notorious) for its stubborn
resistance to linguistic imports.

We cannot predict, then, what may be made an object of
borrowing, but must allow for the possibility of anything's being
borrowed. Nor can we know beforehand whether a language will
be resistant to borrowing, or to what degree. Nor can we establish general laws about the direction in which borrowings will
move. They may pass from culturally inferior to culturally supe-
rior populations or vice versa, from languages with few speakers
to languages with many or vice versa, from the language of subject peoples to the language of their rulers or vice versa, from
dialect to standard language or from standard language to dialect. Wherever two linguistic communities are in contact, the
possibility of borrowing must be taken into account.

In establishing the fact of borrowing, then, the linguist is
generally reduced to using purely linguistic criteria, of which the
most important is the fact that the words involved constitute
counter-examples to the element-functions. We have seen above
that Celtic corresponds with zero to IE *\*p*, Lat. *p*, and that, for
example, the Irish correspondent to Eng. *fish*, Lat. *piscis*, is *iasc*
(p. 18). Now when we discover that the Welsh word for 'fish' is
*pysg*, we must conclude that it is a borrowing from Latin. In
this case, as it happens, the assumption can be supported on
many sides, because we know that in general there was a considerable influence of Latin culture in Wales. It often occurs that
at a given period borrowings between two languages move pre-
dominantly in one direction. A general movement of loan words
that played a great role in Europe proceeds from the Mediterranean countries, especially from the Semitic languages, and
passes through Greek and on to Latin, from Latin to French,
and finally on to Germanic. The English word *sack* has come to

us by this long route. Danish, as we have seen, acquired a large
number of borrowings from Low German at a certain period.
English has a tremendous number of borrowings, partly from
French and partly from Scandinavian. Over a long span of time,
French has borrowed extensively from Latin. Vilhelm Thomsen
showed (particularly in his dissertation of 1869) that Finnish—
which we have seen to be quite conservative in historical times
with respect to admitting foreign lexical material—must in prehistoric times have accepted a very considerable number of loan
words, especially from the Germanic languages. Some of these
borrowings are closer in form to the Common Germanic word
formulæ than anything in the recorded Germanic languages, so
they play a special role in comparative Germanic linguistics.

## II 2. Tabu

The word *tabu* is Polynesian and refers to the situation in which
a word or name can be used in a community only under special
conditions, whether only by certain persons or only in certain
circumstances. This phenomenon was first observed among prim-
itive peoples, whose religious notions often cause it to be very
widespread. Recent investigation, however, has shown that
tabu is known in all societies and at all times, and that it plays
a quite considerable role in our own languages. The most obvious
example is the fact that it is considered improper to name by
name phenomena connected with sexual life or the digestive
process. This tabu is not, as one might perhaps think, common
to all mankind. It is linked to certain societies and is unknown in
many societies outside modern Europe; it did not exist in ancient
Greece. But other areas of life—the religious area, for example—
may also be surrounded by such linguistic mystery: one must
not take God's name in vain. Consequently, if a person has to
mention such things, he must either use allusions and circumlocutions or else simply change the words that designate them.
Often, as is well known, a foreign word is used: it is not the
thing itself that is under tabu, but the sign, and if one uses a

foreign sign, the odium disappears. Or another word is arbitrarily chosen which actually means something quite different but whose external form resembles that of the tabu word enough to call it to mind (*sewer-pipe* for *suicide*). Or, finally—and this will be of special interest to us here—the word is arbitrarily transformed. This can be done in many different ways: by abbreviation (for example *TB* may be used instead of *tuberculosis* to avoid invoking the dreaded disease by using its real name), or by transposition of elements (Dan. *pokker* 'the deuce, the devil', if so derived from *kopper* 'smallpox', can be explained only by tabu, and not as a metathesis, since it runs counter to the general law governing metathesis; see p. 50), or by substitutions of different elements at certain places in the word. One may perhaps, for the purpose of giving an example, be allowed to observe that it can be regarded as permissible in Danish to refer to a little natural business by the verb *nisse*. This word uses *n* to replace the *t* of another word, which is under a fairly strong tabu, although the word with *t*, in turn, was originally introduced as an arbitrary substitute for a third word, which (like the corresponding English word) is under even stronger tabu. In this way, tabu produces counter-examples to the element-functions. There can often be mutual reinforcement by tabu and the action of elements. The transformation of Lat. *meretrīx* 'harlot' to *meletrīx* (*\*meltrīce* is presupposed by older Fr. *meautris*, Provençal *meltritz*) can be explained by a dissimilation like that found in *pelegrīnus*; but the form *menetrīx*, in which the word also appears, cannot be so explained within the framework of the Latin sound system and must be owing to tabu.

## II 3. Neologism

Finally, we must observe that it is, of course, also possible to introduce into a language completely new signs which are neither transformations nor derivations based on other signs but which follow the rules of syllable formation in the linguistic structure. Here again, different linguistic communities at different periods behave quite differently. Most Western European languages, as compared with other language areas, show surprisingly little inclination to accept such neologisms. Rather, our languages betray an aversion to them, if we leave out of account onomatopoetic formations and the special license sometimes granted to creative writers. On the other hand, this need not always be so. To take a particularly striking example from recent times, several thousand new words were arbitrarily introduced into Estonian by government decree in this century, words that were truly created, so to speak, out of nothing, by putting Estonian expression elements together in new ways according to Estonian rules of syllable formation.

Such neologisms, of course, can never be more than apparent counter-examples to the element-functions. A newly created word may perplex the investigator of genetic relationship only if it is fairly close in form to what he might be led by the element-functions to expect to find in the language. The linguist must therefore also be on the watch for this possibility. Moreover, he must keep in mind that if relatively few words in a language (like Greek, for example) can be explained genetically, this need not always be due to borrowing but may also be due to neologistic creation.

# Language Families

The method we have outlined has made possible the recognition of a large number of language families all over the world. As we have already seen, however, there are families of different degrees, so in what follows we shall reserve the term *family* to designate a large family, like Indo-European. Such a family may then be divided into *groups*, *subgroups*, *branches*, and so on. We shall now proceed to a summary review of the most important language families that have so far been established.

I.  The *Indo-European* family (see p. 10)
    1. The *Germanic* group
        A. The *East Germanic* subgroup
            a. The *Gothic* branch, which included several languages, only one of which is at all well recorded (see p. 11).
            b. The *Scandinavian* (or *Norse*) branch. The oldest stage is *Old Norse*, which, as represented in runic inscriptions, is altogether the oldest and most archaic of all the Germanic languages. The younger stage divides into two subbranches: *West Scandinavian* (*Icelandic, Faeroese, Norwegian*) and *East Scandinavian* (*Swedish, Danish*). From 1530 to 1814, Danish was also the standard and literary language of Norway. The Norwegian "riksmål" or "bokmål," is a Danish slightly colored with Norwegian; the "landsmål," a standard language formed on the basis

of the West Norwegian dialect of Søndmøre, has been given equal official status with the "riksmål" since 1892 and provides the foundation for "nynorsk." In 1938 a third standard language, "samnorsk," was introduced as a compromise.

B. The *West Germanic* subgroup

    *a.* The *Anglo-Frisian* branch (*English*, introduced into England by invaders from the Continent and diffused throughout the British Empire and the United States; *Frisian*, spoken along the west coast of North Holland and Germany).

    *b.* The *Dutch-German* branch (*Dutch*, with two written languages: Dutch-Flemish, in Holland, Belgium, and colonies, and Afrikaans, in South Africa; *Low German* and *High German*—see p. 24).

Within Indo-European, languages of the Germanic group presently count the largest number of speakers—a good 400 million, of whom by far the most speak English, the world's most widespread language after Chinese.

2. The *Celtic* group

A. The *Gaelic* subgroup (*Irish; Scottish Gaelic*, introduced into Scotland by Irish immigrants in the fifth century; *Manx*, now extinct, once spoken on the Isle of Man).

B. The *Brythonic* subgroup

    *a.* The *Continental* branch (*Gaulish*, attested by inscriptions, extinct after the conquest of Gaul and the creation of the Roman Empire).

    *b.* The *Insular* branch (*Welsh*, in Wales; *Cornish*, in Cornwall, extinct; *Breton*, introduced into Brittany from Britain in the fifth and sixth centuries, with four different written languages).

3. The *Italic* group

A. The *East Italic* subgroup, considerably more wide-

spread than West Italic at the beginning of historical times.

 *a.* The *Umbro-Samnite* branch (*Umbrian*, in the
Italian region of Umbria; *Samnite*, in southern
Italy, with the official language called *Oscan*).

 *b.* The *Lepontic* branch (in the northwestern Alps).

B. The *West Italic* subgroup

 *a.* The *Sicilian* branch

 *b.* The *Continental* branch, including, among several
languages of small diffusion, *Latin*, in western-
most Latium, by the mouth of the Tiber and in
the city of Rome. Except for Latin, which was
to flourish as few other languages have, all the
Italic languages died out before the end of antiquity and are known only through inscriptions.
At the beginning of historical times, Latin was
spoken over an area smaller than Zealand in
Denmark, and it came to dominate half a con-
tinent. At the close of antiquity, it was continued in the *Romance* languages, under which
form it can be divided into six subbranches: (1)
*Italo-Sardinian* (*Italian*, on the Italian penin-
sula, in Sicily, and, to some degree, in Corsica;
*Sardinian*, in Sardinia and, to a certain extent,
in Corsica); (2) *Hispano-Romance* (*Spanish*, in
the greater part of Spain, in northwestern Africa,
in all of America south of the United States except for Brazil, and in the Philippine Islands;
*Portuguese*, in Portugal, Brazil, the Azores, and
Madeira; *Galician*, in northwestern Spain); (3)
*Gallo-Romance* (*Catalan*, principally in Catalonia
and southeastern France; *Provençal*, in southern
France; *French*, the official language of France
and some former colonies, and one of the official
languages (with Flemish) of Belgium, (with

German, Italian, and Rhæto-Romance) of
Switzerland, (with English) of Canada, and
(with German) of Luxemburg); (4) *Rhæto-Romance* (in southeastern Switzerland and northeastern Italy); (5) *Dalmatian* (in Dalmatia,
extinct since the nineteenth century); and (6)
*Rumanian* (in Rumania, with the partial exception of southeasternmost Transylvania, with
diffusion into the Balkans).

4. The *Hellenic* group
   A. The *Macedonian* subgroup, comprising only one
   extinct and poorly known language.
   B. The *Greek* subgroup, also comprising only one language.

5. The *Baltic* group
   A. The *North Baltic* subgroup (*Lithuanian* and *Lettish*).
   Lithuanian is the only living language that is immediately explicable from the Common Indo-
   European system of formulæ.
   B. The *South Baltic* subgroup, comprising several languages, of which only one is attested—*Old Prussian*,
   which died out in the seventeenth century, dis-
   lodged by German speakers who took over the name
   of the Baltic Prussians.

6. The *Slavic* group
   A. The *South Slavic* subgroup
      *a.* The *Bulgarian* branch (one language) and
      *Macedonian* (also one language, an older stage of
      which, in the form of *Old Church Slavic*, is the
      oldest attested Slavic language).
      *b.* The *Jugoslav* branch (*Serbo-Croatian* to the east,
      *Slovene* to the west).
   B. The *West Slavic* subgroup (*Sorbian*—also called
   *Lusatian* or *Wendish*—with two literary forms, the
   language of the Wends, in Lower and Upper Lusatia;

    *Polabian*, around the Elbe (Slavic *Laba*) and in Hanover, extinct since the eighteenth century; *Polish; Czech* and *Slovak*).

  C. The *Russian*, or *East Slavic*, subgroup (*Great Russian, Ukrainian, White Russian*).

7. The *Albanian* group (comprising only one language).
8. The *Armenian* group (comprising only one language).
9. The *Iranian* group

  A. The *West Iranian* subgroup (*Persian* in three stages: *Old Persian* in cuneiform inscriptions, *Pehlevi*, and *Modern Persian*, the official language of Iran; *Avestan*, indigenous in ancient times to the region north of Old Persian, attested in the writings of the religious leader Zarathustra, closely related to the younger *Chaldean Pehlevi*, and later extinct; *Kurdish*, in and around the mountain region on the border between Turkey and Iran; several other languages, including some in various regions of Iran).

  B. The *East Iranian* subgroup (*Sogdian*, attested in texts from Chinese Turkestan, continued in the modern *Yagnobi*, which is spoken in the northwest of the Pamir, east of Lake Aral; *Sakian*, in texts found in Chinese Turkestan; *Afghan*, or *Pushtu; Ossetic*, in the Caucasus; various other languages, including those of the Pamir and Baluchistan).

10. The *Indic* group. *Old Indic* comprises two dialects: *Vedic* (found in the Vedas) and *Sanskrit*. The *Middle Indic* languages are referred to under the general name of *Prākrits* and include *Pāli*, the sacred language of Southern Buddhism. *Modern Indic* comprises a very large number of languages (including *Romany*, the language of the Gypsies), spoken by some 400 million people. At the present time, Indic follows Germanic in number of speakers; next comes Romance, with about 370 million, and next Slavic, with about 270 million.

11. *Hittite*, an ancient language discovered only in recent times, recorded partly in hieroglyphic texts but mainly in cuneiform; indigenous to Asia Minor in the fifteenth century before our era.

12. *Tokharian*, discovered early in the present century, spoken in Chinese Turkestan in the seventh century of our era.

To the Indo-European family also belong some linguistic remnants (i.e. fragmentarily attested dead languages) of the Mediterranean region: *Messapic, Venetic, Thracian, Phrygian,* and *Lycian*.

II. The *Hamito-Semitic* family
　1. The *Hamitic* group
　　A. The *Egyptian* subgroup, recorded in hieroglyphic inscriptions from the fourth millennium before our era. Younger stages are *demotic Egyptian* and *Coptic*, which died and was replaced by Arabic in the sixteenth century of our era.
　　B. The *Libyco-Berber* subgroup (extinct in Libya, replaced mainly by Arabic; modern languages in Algeria, Tunis, Morocco, and the Sahara).
　　C. The *Cushitic* subgroup (eastern Nubia, Ethiopia, Somalia, East Africa).
　2. The *Semitic* group
　　A. The *Akkadian* subgroup, comprising only one language—the ancient language of Iraq, recorded in cuneiform.
　　B. The *West Semitic* subgroup
　　　*a.* The *Northwest Semitic* branch comprises two subbranches: *Canaanite* (*Old Canaanite, Moabite, Hebrew, Phoenician*) and *Aramaic*. With the exception of Hebrew and a few remaining dialects of East Aramaic, all these languages are extinct. Hebrew, to be sure, died out in Palestine as a spoken language in the third century before

## Abbreviations

| | |
|---|---|
| Al. | Algonkin |
| Ar. | Arawak |
| Aus. | Australian |
| Ba. | Basque |
| Bu. | Bushman |
| C. | Caucasian languages |
| Car. | Carib |
| Chu. | Chukchi |
| Cu. | Cushitic |
| Dr. | Dravidian |
| Du. | Dutch |
| Eng. | English |
| Esk. | Eskimo |
| Fr. | French |
| F.-U. | Finno-Ugrian |
| Gi. | Gilyak |
| H. | Hungarian |
| Ham. | Hamitic |
| Ho. | Hottentot |
| I.-E. | Indo-European |
| Iroq. | Iroquois |
| Jap. | Japanese |
| Ka. | Kamchadal |
| Kh. | Khmer |
| Ko. | Korean |
| Kor. | Koryak |
| Mo. | Mon |
| Mu. | Munda |
| Pa. | Papuan |
| Port. | Portuguese |
| Sem. | Semitic |
| Sp. | Spanish |
| Ta. | Tasmanian |
| T.-G. | Tupi-Guaraní |
| Tib.-Bur. | Tibeto-Burman |
| Viet. | Vietnamese |
| Yuk. | Yukagir |

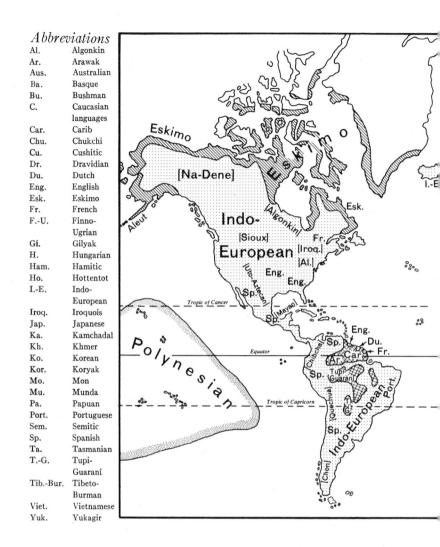

MAP OF LANGUAGES OF THE WORLD

Names within square brackets indicate languages not belonging to th
group which is dominant in the area.

Patterns serve only to distinguish bordering language-groups. Thus, tw

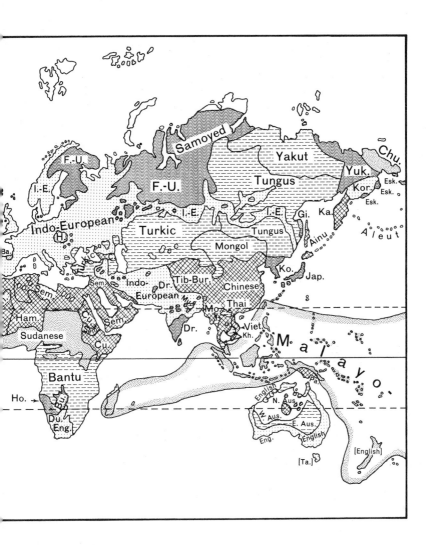

nguages shown in the same pattern do not necessarily belong to the same
roup. In case of doubt concerning linguistic relationship, the reader should
onsult the chapter on "Language Families."

our era and was replaced by Aramaic, but it continued to be a language of learning and religion, and it also found continuation in Yiddish, which can be viewed as a blend of Hebrew and High German. Moreover, Hebrew has been reintroduced as a living language, *Modern Hebrew*, in present-day Israel.

b. The *Southwest Semitic* branch comprises three subbranches: *Arabic* (which, as vehicle of Mohammedan culture, has been the most widely diffused of all the Hamito-Semitic languages; with English and Chinese, one of the most widespread modern cultural languages; spoken in modern times in Arabia, Iraq, Syria, Egypt, northwest Africa, and Malta), *South Arabic*, and *Ethiopic* (including seven modern languages, of which the best known is *Amharic*, the official language of Ethiopia).

III. The *Bantu* family (from *ba-ntu*, plural of *mu-ntu* 'human being'), comprising a very large number of native languages in the whole southern half of Africa except for the southwestern corner.

IV. The *Uralic* family
1. The *Samoyed* group, comprising five languages along the western part of the northern coast of the Soviet Union. Two of them acquired the status of literary languages in 1930.
2. The *Finno-Ugrian* group
   A. The *Ugrian* subgroup
      a. The *Ob-Ugrian* branch (*Ostyak*, on the river Ob'; *Vogul*, to the west of Ostyak, in the Ural mountains; both languages acquired literary status in 1930).
      b. The *Hungarian* branch (one language only, the

official language of Hungary; also spoken in scattered parts of Slovakia and Jugoslavia).

B. The *Lapp* subgroup (one language only, but including six quite markedly divergent dialect groups, in Norway, Sweden, Finland, and the Soviet Union).

C. The *Finno-Permian* subgroup

 *a.* The *Permian* branch (*Komi*, or *Zyrian*, in the Komi ASSR, in the northeastern corner of European Russia, with a rich literature from the fourteenth century; *Udmurt*, or *Votyak*, in the Udmurt ASSR, northeast of Kazan').

 *b.* The *Finno-Mordvin* branch, comprising three subbranches: (1) *Mordvin*, a language spoken in scattered areas around the Volga between the cities of Gorky (formerly Nizhny Novgorod) and Kuybyshev (formerly Samara); (2) *Mari*, or *Cheremiss*, one language only, in the Mari ASSR (north of Kazan') and in scattered areas east of the Udmurt ASSR; (3) *Baltic Finnish*, comprising ten quite closely related languages, of which the best known are *Finnish*, *Karelian*, and *Estonian*.

V.  The *Altaic* family

 1. The *Turkic* group, comprising *Turkish*, or *Osmanli*, in Turkey, in northern Syria, and in scattered areas of northern Greece and of Serbia; and a number of other languages up and down the Soviet Union—including the official language of Azerbaidjan, of the Tatar ASSR, and of the Chuvash ASSR (*Chuvash*) and *Yakut*, along the lower Lena—as well as in Sin-Kiang Province in Chinese Turkestan. The *Old Turkic* of the Orkhon inscriptions in Outer Mongolia was deciphered by Vilhelm Thomsen in 1893 and became the basis for the genetic comparison of the Turkic languages.

 2. The *Mongol* group, comprising a number of languages.

mainly in Mongolia and the adjacent region of Siberia, together with parts of Kuku-nor Province. Literature dates from the thirteenth century.

3. The *Tungus* group (*Evenki*, in the greater part of Siberia east of the Yenisei, a literary language since 1930; *Manchu*, in Manchu-Kuo and the Soviet Dal'ne-Vostochny Kray (between Nikolayevsk and Vladivostok), with literature beginning in the twelfth century).

VI. The *Sino-Austric* family
1. The *Thai-Chinese* group, comprising *Chinese*, the language spoken by the greatest number of people in the world (600 million), and the *Thai* languages of Indo-China, of which the best known is *Siamese*, the official language of Thailand.
2. The *Tibeto-Burman* group.
3. The *Austric* group
   A. The *Malayo-Polynesian* subgroup (Pacific islands, Malaya, Madagascar; Indonesia; the old cultural language of Java).
   B. The *Austro-Asiatic* subgroup, comprising three branches: the *Munda* languages of India, especially in Bihar Province (the best known of these languages is *Santālī*), the *Mon-Khmer* languages of Indo-China, and *Vietnamese*.

Although we have used *family* as the most inclusive term for a large class of genetically related languages, there is, of course, nothing to prevent something we have called a family from being related to other languages. For one thing, it is possible to prove that two languages are genetically related, but it is never possible to prove that two languages are *not* genetically related. We use the term *family*, therefore, for the largest class of related languages that we can set up at a given stage of our research. In this respect, family is a relative term, and if two families are set up which are later found to be genetically related, we should, if you will, call them one family, each of them a group, and so on. But this would usually be impractical. Even though, for example, we now know that the Indo-European languages are genetically related to other languages, we still continue to speak of the Indo-European family, and we may very well do so, provided only that we admit the possibility of there being *families of families.*

In each case, it will be merely a practical question whether we change our terms or not. For a long time, what we have called the Sino-Austric family was seen as five different families having no demonstrated genetic relationship: (1) Sino-Tibetan, comprising Thai-Chinese and Tibeto-Burman, (2) Malayo-Polynesian, (3) Munda, (4) Mon-Khmer, (5) Vietnamese. In 1889 the German linguist Ernst Kuhn demonstrated that the last three are related, and in 1908–10 the Danish linguist Kurt Wulff was able to show their relationship to Malayo-Polynesian. Much later, the genetic relationship between Austric and Sino-Tibetan was finally demonstrated in a posthumous work of Wulff's. We have drawn the consequences from this and combined all these groups into one family, because the genetic relationships that Wulff demonstrated contradict the older classification: the relationship between Thai-Chinese and Austric has been shown to be closer than that between Thai-Chinese and Tibeto-Burman, so there is no longer any basis for maintaining a separate Sino-Tibetan family.

A genetic relationship between Indo-European and Hamito-Semitic was demonstrated in detail by the Danish linguist Hermann Møller, using the method of element-functions, in studies dating from 1906–17. Later, by the same method, the French Africanist Mlle Lilias Homburger thought it possible to demonstrate genetic relationship between Hamito-Semitic and Bantu and even conjectured adding to the family both some northeastern (Nilotic) and some western Sudanese languages, of which the northeastern seem to be nearer than Coptic to Old Egyptian and demotic Egyptian. And there can be no doubt of the genetic relationship between Indo-European and Uralic after Holger Pedersen's success in demonstrating a number of element-correspondences.

By combining these far-reaching results we may perhaps reduce the six families listed above to three: (1) *Nostratic* (a name proposed by Holger Pedersen for the languages related to our own, from Lat. *nostrās* 'our fellow countryman'), comprising, so far as we can see at present, Indo-European, Hamito-Semitic, Uralic, and possibly Bantu (together with the Sudanese languages mentioned above); (2) *Sino-Austric*; (3) *Altaic*.

The language families discussed here are the only language classes of any considerable size to have been established as families by the method of element-functions. The same method has been applied to the families of families that we have talked about in the last paragraph, but because the great syntheses involved are so recent, we must prudently admit that proof has not yet been given, even in those instances where there is no doubt that it will be.

Taken together, the languages we have listed above are spoken by about eight-ninths of the world's present population. But linguistics must, of course, be concerned with dead languages as well as the living.

The remaining languages of the world constitute an enormous number of genetically isolated speech communities or families of quite restricted size. Examples are Japanese, Korean, Ainu in northern Japan,* the Palæo-Asiatic languages of northeastern Siberia (a purely geographical classification), South Caucasian (a true language family), North Caucasian (rather a purely geographical classification of a very large number of scattered languages), Dravidian (in southern India, a true family), the Australian languages (merely a geographical classification), the

---

* According to recent investigations, Ainu would appear to be an Indo-European language.

non-Bantu languages of the Sudan, the Khoin family in southwest Africa (Bushman and Hottentot), Basque (an isolated language on the French-Spanish border), Eskimo (together with Aleut), and, finally, the extraordinarily numerous American Indian languages, which are still classified into no fewer than some hundred different families. To these may further be added a number of isolated linguistic remains, principally in the Near East and the Mediterranean region (for example, Sumerian in Iraq, and Etruscan in Italy).

# Parent Languages

We have given an operational definition of genetic relationship above (p. 30) and shown that it consists in what we have called element-functions, constant correspondences between the systems of expression elements in the related languages. Genetic relationship is demonstrated by the demonstration of such element-functions, and in no other way. A superficial similarity between languages or between signs in different languages plays no role in genetic relationship or in its demonstration. Such "similarity" cannot be used as a scientific criterion, if only because a feeling that things are similar is a purely subjective matter (cf. above, p. 43). In many instances, two signs can be shown to be genetically related even though most people would perhaps find no resemblance between them. Such forms as the nominative singular *hayr* in Armenian and *patḗr* in Greek, or the genitive singular *hawr* in Armenian and *patrós* in Greek, would probably not generally be taken as having the least external resemblance, yet they can be shown, on the basis of element-functions, to be photographically identical. On the other hand, two signs may bear a strong resemblance without having any genetic relationship whatsoever. Primary examples of this are most loan words, and if we should attempt to base our constructions on external similarity, it would be impossible to distinguish between borrowed and genetically related words. But of course there are also instances of two signs in different languages resembling each other by pure accident: 'big' is *dìdis* in Lithuanian and *didi* in Georgian, but the two languages are genetically unrelated and the two words have nothing to do with each other; to *call* is *kaleîn* in Greek, but these cannot be the same word since Gr. *k* in this position corresponds genetically to Gmc. *h* (cf. *kúōn* and *hound*, *he-katón* and *hund-red*, etc.).

Now if we ask for the cause of this element-function that we have called genetic relationship between two languages, we see that it can be accounted for only on the assumption that the two languages have a common origin. This is the only conceivable explanation, so we are logically compelled to accept this consequence of genetic relationship. Genetic relationship consists in a connexion between the expression elements and signs of the two languages, and the reason for this connexion must necessarily be that the expression elements and signs of the two languages are later developments of older expression elements and signs that were common to the two languages, or, in other words, that the two languages developed from the splitting of a single *basic language* (commonly called *parent language*). Thus (according to the classification given in the preceding chapter), behind Danish and Swedish there must lie an East Scandinavian parent language, behind this and West Scandinavian a Scandinavian parent language, behind this and Gothic an East Germanic parent language, behind this and West Germanic a Germanic parent language, behind this and the other Indo-European language groups an Indo-European parent language, and behind this and the language families that are genetically related to Indo-European a Nostratic parent language. Now we have a solid ground of reality under our feet, and we can supplement our earlier operational definition of genetic relationship with a *"real" definition: Genetic relationship between two languages means that they have developed from a single basic, or parent, language.*

All that we can know with any certainty about the parent language is what we can read from the formulæ we have established on the basis of genetic comparison of languages. In no instance has the parent language been transmitted to us; we *reconstruct* it from the element-functions. The parent language that we presuppose for the Romance languages may well be called Latin, because we can conclude from our knowledge of history that it *must* have been Latin which, by splitting, developed into the Romance languages. But, as we have already noted (p. 22), the parent language that we are led to reconstruct for Romance is not the same Latin as the Latin that we know from the transmitted literature.

The expression elements and parts of words (almost never whole words; see p. 27) that we set up in our formulæ must, then, be ascribed to the parent language. They are fragments of a language that we know in no other way. And here it is very important to realize clearly how much and how little real content we have a right to read into our formulæ—in other words, what we know with certainty and what we do not know with certainty about the parent language:

A. We know with certainty
   1. that such a language existed;
   2. that the language contained in its structure the expression elements represented by our element-formulæ (provided, of course, these formulæ have been correctly set up—not a completely superfluous proviso, as we shall shortly see);
   3. that these expression elements in the structure were defined by the possibilities of combination that are implied in our formulæ for signs.
B. We do not know with certainty
   1. where, when, or by whom the language was used, or whether it was ever used (one possibility to be reckoned with is that it was never used, but was transformed from the very start in the directions implied by the several languages under comparison);
   2. whether it contained in its structure more expression elements than those designated by our element-formulæ;
   3. whether the expression elements we know to have been in the language were defined in the structure by more possibilities of combination than those implied in our formulæ for signs;
   4. how the linguistic usage (if there was one; see point 1) of the language was organized and, in particular, (a) what

whole words or sentences were, or could be, used, (b) how the expression elements were represented in speech, in writing, or in other ways, and (c) what meaning was contained in the signs.

In these last four respects, where we have no certainty, we may, if we wish, contruct *hypotheses* based on probabilities. It cannot be denied that such hypotheses are extraordinarily tempting and that, to a certain extent, they arise quite naturally. Here we have a happy hunting ground for romantically disposed and imaginative spirits. By combining probability and fantasy, we can conjure up a whole picture of a prehistoric language like the Indo-European parent language, with words and sentences and a definite pronunciation and definite word-meanings, constructed to "resemble" as closely as possible words, sentences, pronunciations, and meanings in the historically known languages. And from this, another picture can be conjured up of a whole prehistoric society and prehistoric culture, all based on conjectures about what words existed and what things they designated. And, still hypothetically, this prehistoric society can be assigned some definite place or other on the basis of conjectures, say, about the plants and animals that might have been designated by the words in the language. Naturally, science has not refrained from constructing and discussing such hypotheses, quite justifiably—so long as it is remembered that they can never be anything but hypotheses. Classical linguistics, however, was well on the way to making such hypothesis-spinning the essential part of genetic comparison and thereby contributed to bringing it into unjust discredit as an insecure and hypothetical science. It is just the opposite. It is a science with secure results and an exact method. But it can maintain itself as such only by keeping clear of the hypothetical domain, cleaving to what is known with certainty, and respecting the limitations of its method.

In no way does the method permit us to infer culture, people, or "race" from language. The fact that our language is Indo-European can, of course—if we care to use an inappropriate wording—be expressed by saying that we are Indo-Europeans. But no other meaning can be correctly attached to this sentence than that our language is connected with other Indo-European languages by element-functions. This means that the system of elements in our language and bits of its words go back to an earlier, purely linguistic, Indo-European unity, but it in no way means that we ourselves go back to some unity connected with it. Precisely because languages can spread and move and be transferred to quite different populations from their original speakers (as Latin, starting from the little area by the mouth of the Tiber, was disseminated over an enormous number of populations differing greatly in all respects, or as, in more recent times, English has spread to many quarters of the world), it is impossible to maintain any such connexion between languages and peoples. There is not even any certainty that the possibly quite small population that spoke a language thousands of years ago (like, for example, the small band of Latin-speaking men by the mouth of the Tiber) actually has any direct descendants now or, if it does, that those descendants speak a language genetically continuing the language of their ancestors. This element of uncertainty obviously becomes greater the more language families are involved and, consequently, the farther back we may go into prehistory in our hypothetical dating of the parent language. Linguistic arguments, therefore, cannot be used to support racial theories.

As we have seen, the element-functions are set up without regard for the way the elements are represented in the languages under consideration (whether, for example, by letters or by sounds), and the element-formulæ must therefore likewise have an abstract character. It is certainly true that the elements we compare in the different Indo-European languages, for example, are represented by letters: after all, in the case of dead languages like Ancient Greek and Latin, Old Indic, and Gothic, we have

nothing but written characters to deal with and can only construct more or less probable hypotheses about their pronunciation. But if we do not argue from the letters of these languages
that the Indo-European parent language also had letters, it is
not merely because we happen to know that the Greek and
Latin alphabets (and the Indic) are transformations of the
Semitic alphabet and consequently have a non–Indo-European
origin. Rather, it is above all because our method simply will not
permit us to say anything whatsoever about how the elements of
the parent language were represented. The same is of course
true (one might be tempted to say, to an even higher degree)
when it comes to the representation of elements by certain
sounds in pronunciation. In this matter, only hypotheses can—
and no hypotheses need—be offered. Such hypotheses may have
a greater or lesser degree of probability, but it is always a
question of probability only, never of certainty. The hypothesis
that IE *m* was pronounced approximately like our *m* has a very
high degree of probability; the probability that IE *ᴀ was pronounced approximately like the last vowel in our word *sofa*
(one of the hypotheses that have been suggested) is very low.
It is therefore unfortunate that classical linguistics called the
element-functions *sound laws* and, for example, called the con-
sonant-functions discovered by Rask for Germanic (p. 19) and
High German (p. 24) the Germanic and High German *sound
shifts* (Rask himself called them *letter changes*, a considerably
more honest and sober term).

In the same way, specifications of meaning for the words (or,
better, the parts of words) of the parent language remain hypothetical and, like specifications of pronunciation, are superfluous
and irrelevant from the point of view of the theory. Here too,
the degree of probability can be greater or less. Languages
seldom show such agreement with respect to meaning as they
may show with respect to the pronunciation of an element
(where the pronunciation in the several languages is known or
can be determined with a high degree of probability); very

rarely do we find such unanimity over the meaning of a word as we have over the pronunciation of the element *\*m*. It might be thought that there is a high degree of probability in the assumption that IE *\*pAtér* meant 'father'. But in the first place, *\*pAtér* is composed of a root *\*pA-* and a derivational suffix *\*-t-r*, which contains yet a third component, the vowel *\*ē* that alternates with *\*ō* (see p. 29). The root *\*pA-* is in regular alternation with another form, *\*pō-*, which appears in many Indo-European languages (e.g. in OI *pắ-ti* 'he protects') with meanings like 'protect', etc. The suffix *\*-t-r* is known from many other words. In the several Indo-European languages it designates the person who carries out an action (e.g. Gr. *rhḗ-tōr* 'speaker', Lat. *ōrā-tor*). In other words, *\*pA-tér* is a regular formation that we might expect most probably to have meant something like 'the protector'. It need not have existed in the parent language; it is so regular and obvious that it could have been formed independently in the several Indo-European languages at an early date. And whether or not it belonged to the parent language, there is nothing to indicate that its original meaning was 'father'.

One reason why the content of meaning must necessarily remain hypothetical is that, as a rule, we are not able to reconstruct whole words but only *minimal signs*, i.e. the smallest word-components (such as roots, suffixes, and flexional endings) that can be shown to be meaningful in various languages. The moment we are faced with a formation of regular type in Indo-European, we have to admit the possibility of its having arisen at any time, in the parent language or later, just as the English ending *-er*, denoting an agent, can be freely added to any verb, even if it never has been before. Corresponding to the Danish verb *leje* 'to hire' (Goth. *leihwan*) we find Gr. *leípein* 'to leave'. The Greek present *leípō* is to be understood as IE *\*leík₃-ō*. In Latin, the present is *linquō*, equaling IE *\*li-n-k₃-ō* (in which the *\*e* of the root is alternating with zero—see p. 29—and an *n*-component has been infixed into the root). In Old Indic, the present of the same verb is *riṇắcmi*, equaling IE *\*li-nḗ-k₃-mi* (with a different ending, -*mi*, for the first person singular and with a different alternation grade in the infixed component). Now all these formations represent *possible* types of present formations for such a verb in Indo-European, but we cannot say which of them was used in the parent language—possibly none, possibly one or more.

Thus we reconstruct, not words, but parts of words, and without knowing their pronunciation or their meaning. This might seem to be pitifully little—but in fact it is a very great deal. By using the little information that we have, we can prove genetic relationships within very broad, indeed unlimited, linguistic domains; and we can say a lot about the structure of the parent language and thereby explain a great number of details in the various languages belonging to the family. The method even permits us to *predict*. It permits us, for example, to infer with certainty that if the word *mother* existed in Gothic, and if it was not subjected to action of elements, analogical transformation, abbreviation, or tabu, it must have been *modar*—of that we can be quite certain. In other words, reconstruction can be reversed, and we can thus construct for ourselves the form that a word must have had in the individual languages within the language family. Such reconstruction is, in fact, one of the prerequisites for distinguishing between borrowings and genetically related words, as well as between element-functions and counter-examples.

Genetic linguistics may therefore be called absolutely exact, and is perhaps the most exact domain of the humanities.

As we have already noted, only a minority of the words in a language can, in whole or in part, be shown to have genetic connexions with words in related languages—whether because of new formations, borrowings, or transformations. Only within this small sector of the vocabulary can genetic linguistics use the method of element-functions. It is therefore quite impossible for genetic linguistics to account for all the words in a language by means of its exact method. Even if we must always try to explain as many words as possible in this way, always respecting the element-functions, genetic linguistics can only to a very limited extent give an unambiguous and certain answer to questions about *etymologies*, i.e. the individual histories of particular words. In most cases this is an extremely complicated problem, without any unambiguous solution, for which the method of genetic linguistics is inadequate. An etymological dictionary sets itself the tempting, but in fact unscientific, task of accounting for *all* the words in a language. In doing so, it strains the method far beyond its powers and brings unmerited discredit on it. In order to estimate the probability of the etymological hypotheses such a dictionary offers for the origin of a word, one must first know the element-functions within the language family concerned, so as to be able to see whether the hypotheses agree with them. A layman who has not studied the element-functions cannot, in fact, use an etymological dictionary with reasonable and fair judgment.

# Typological Relationship
## of Languages

We observed earlier that it should be possible to set up functions between languages other than the element-functions. In addition to being ordered into families, languages may be ordered into linguistic *types*, according to their structure. Such classification depends, of course, on what structural features are used as criteria. Just as men can be divided into tall and short, white, black, yellow, and red, dark-haired and blond, etc., so the universe of languages can be divided in a number of different ways, depending on one's point of view. One possible choice is between classification according to linguistic structure and classification according to linguistic usage, with various bases for further division under each case.

The only linguistic typology to achieve a place in classical linguistics was a classification according to linguistic usage. The central point of interest was the structure of signs, especially of words. *Words* are permutable signs, signs that can exchange places within a linguistic chain: *softly answered* consists of two words, because one can also say *answered softly*; *soft-ly* and *answer-ed* each consist of two signs, but these signs cannot be put in another order. Permutable signs attracted an extraordinary amount of attention from classical linguistics, beginning with antiquity, since it was thought, in connexion with Aristotelian conceptual logic, that each such sign stood for one concept. This also explains the interest that has been felt in dividing the universe of languages according to the word structure chosen by the linguistic usage.

As a rule, four linguistic types have been distinguished:

1. An *isolating* type, in which the words are invariable, not subject to inflexion or derivation, and in which grammatical

relationships can be expressed only by word order (as in English *dog bites man* and *man bites dog*, where different word order alone expresses grammatical relationships expressed in other languages by different cases) or by the addition of independent words (for example, the plural may be expressed by adding the word 'many' to the form that also serves as singular, or the present tense by adding the word 'now'). The example always quoted for this type is Classical Chinese (modern spoken Chinese is a different matter).

2. An *agglutinating* type, in which all grammatical relationships (derivations and inflexions) are expressed by suffixes, signs attached *after* the lexical component or root of the word, with each relationship having its own special suffix. In Turkish, where the suffix *-lar-* expresses the plural, *-a* the dative, *-da* the locative, and *-dan* the ablative, the word *kuş* 'bird' is declined as follows:

|  | singular | plural |
|---|---|---|
| nominative | *kuş* | *kuş-lar* |
| dative | *kuş-a* | *kuş-lar-a* |
| locative | *kuş-da* | *kuş-lar-da* |
| ablative | *kuş-dan* | *kuş-lar-dan* |

The Altaic and Uralic languages are taken as principal examples of this type.

3. An *inflecting* type, in which the boundary between root and suffix is not clear, in which an individual suffix often expresses several different grammatical relationships at once (like Lat. *-ārum* in *bonārum*; see p. 32), and in which the root itself may undergo change during inflexion, with vowel alternations or inserted components. The older Indo-European languages have been taken as models of this type.

4. A *polysynthetic* type, in which all grammatical relationships in the sentence can be expressed by affixes or by alterations of a single root. A sentence often is equivalent to a single word, none of its components being permutable. Greenlandic

has been cited as an example: a sentence like *kavfiliorniaruma-galuarpunga* 'I should like to make coffee' contains only one word.

Many objections have been made to this classification. One of its unsatisfactory features is that the types are almost never found pure, and most languages represent mixtures. The classification was originally set up by Friedrich von Schlegel and Wilhelm von Humboldt. In our times, the American linguist Edward Sapir developed it further, in a very ingenious but extremely complicated way, into a system intended to provide place for all conceivable word structures. In this supplemented and clarified form, the typology of word structure merits consideration. We shall not use Sapir's elaborate schema here, but shall only consider briefly what can be learned by setting up such linguistic types.

Although the original attempt was to identify the linguistic types with certain families—the isolating type with Thai-Chinese, the agglutinating with Altaic and Uralic, the inflecting with Indo-European, and the polysynthetic with certain American languages, for example—it soon became evident that the attempt could not succeed. However linguistic types are set up, they will clearly never coincide with linguistic families. The very fact of linguistic change, which underlies the emergence of language families, implies that a language may change type in the course of time. Even if it can be maintained that Indo-European was once inflexional, many Indo-European languages have now passed over to quite other types, without, of course, ceasing to be Indo-European. An Armenian declensional schema like

|                 | singular          | plural       |
|-----------------|-------------------|--------------|
| nominative      | *hay* 'an Armenian' | *hay-er*     |
| dative-genitive | *hay-u*           | *hay-er-u*   |
| instrumental    | *hay-ov*          | *hay-er-ov*  |
| ablative        | *hay-ē*           | *hay-er-ē*   |

obviously illustrates pure agglutination. It has been supposed that this is due to Turkish influence; however that may be, Armenian, even in its oldest form, no longer belongs to the inflecting type.

Another Indo-European language, Modern English, has, if anything, become isolating in type and in this respect is closer to Chinese than to its genetic origin. The same has been asserted of Modern French by some linguists, but in the opinion of others, that language is instead on the way towards polysynthesis: in the sentence *je ne le lui ai pas donné* 'I didn't give it to him', only one permutation is possible (*ne le lui ai-je pas donné?* 'Didn't I give it to him?'), so we may here be faced with the kind of sentence-words we found in Greenlandic.

Thus, genetic and typological relationship are two quite different things that have nothing to do with each other. Within one and the same family, we can find languages of fundamentally different types, and within one and the same type, languages of fundamentally different families. The two divisions of the universe of languages have nothing in common. They are established on completely different bases and from completely different points of view. In the same way, the zoologist can classify animals systematically as mammals, fish, etc., but also ecologically, setting up, for example, a category of marine animals that would include whales and seals, octopuses, oysters, and fish—animals belonging to quite distinct categories in the systematic classification.

Classical linguistics has been far less interested in typological than in genetic linguistic relationship. But no long reflexion is needed to see that this is a rich and extremely important field, although still almost entirely uncultivated. It would clearly be possible to set up a linguistic typology from many other points of view than the one that was arbitrarily chosen by classical linguistics and that turns out to be the most superficial of all— that of word structure. It is also easy to see that, whatever points of view are chosen, the situation will remain the same:

the resulting classification will cut across the genetic classification and be quite unrelated to it.

When we try to set up a linguistic typology from more penetrating and immanent points of view than have been chosen till now, we soon come to see that the entities which must be compared in the different languages are *categories*. These will be (1) categories in the linguistic structure (like vowels and consonants, accents and modulations, and their various subcategories on the expression side, and grammatical categories like case, gender, and number on the content side) and (2) categories in the linguistic usage (like the expression categories of sounds and the content categories of meanings). From all these points of view, the languages that show the same categories must be assigned to the same linguistic type. Comparison of elements, on the other hand, will never be of interest for linguistic typology, where the fact that two languages have an element in common will always mean that they have a category in common—the category represented by that element. This will come out more clearly from what follows, but we are already in a position to state that this is why genetic relationship and typological relationship remain two essentially different things. Having operationally defined genetic relationship as a function between languages that consists in element-functions, we may give a corresponding *operational definition of typological relationship as a function between languages consisting in the fact that categories in each language have function to categories in each of the others.* Just as genetic relationship is recognized on the basis of element-function, typological relationship, when it penetrates below the most superficial and accidental level (that of word structure), is recognized on the basis of *category-function*.

Such a typology will also naturally account for the structure of the units (syllables, for example) that enter into a language, since the structure of these units depends simply on the categories found in the language. We have defined a category as the sum of the entities that can be inserted at definite places in the chain (p. 33), and we have shown that vowels and consonants are examples of categories (p. 35). A unit like the syllable, then, will depend on the existing categories of elements, and so for all other units.

An exhaustive linguistic typology is, in fact, the biggest and most important task facing linguistics. Unlike linguistic genetics, it has no regional limitations. Its ultimate aim must be to show which linguistic structures are possible, in general, and why it is just those structures, and not others, that are possible. And here it will come closer than any other kind of linguistics to what might be called the problem of the essence of language. Finally, it will prove to be superordinated to genetic linguistics, since only through linguistic typology can we hope to understand what laws govern linguistic change and what possibilities of change a given linguistic type implies. Only through typology does linguistics rise to quite general points of view and become a science. At present, to be sure, very little has been realized of this high hope. The task has been set, but is still far from being accomplished. Classical linguistics has been seriously interested only in usage and genetics, while structure and typology have been left almost completely uncultivated. The central problems have not been solved—have not even been posed—by classical linguistics. This is deplorable, if you will, and the reader may well deplore the fact that the following exposition of linguistic typology will necessarily amount to nothing more than sketchy suggestions—an unrealized program, a questionnaire with unfilled blanks. But for the scholar there is nothing more beautiful than the vision of a science still to be created.

# Types of Linguistic Structure

Since a category consists of the entities that can occupy a given place in the chain, we must start from the chain as the immediate datum in determining the structure of any particular language (état de langue); it is through an analysis of the chain that we arrive at the categories. A whole linguistic chain that is so taken as an object of analysis is called a *text*.

Naturally, the analysis must not be a haphazard chopping up of the text but must be performed with an eye to the *relations* between its constituent parts (see p. 32). These relations may be of several kinds.

First, we have to distinguish between *implicational* and *nonimplicational relations*. We shall say that two entities have an *implicational relation* whenever the presence of one of them in the chain is a necessary presupposition for the presence of the other, or, to put it the other way, whenever one of the entities necessarily implies the other. And we shall speak of a *nonimplicational relation* when there is no such presupposition between the related elements—when we can have either entity present without the other.

*Nonimplicational relation* is very common between elements. In *bland* there is a relation between *b* and *l*: they can appear together in the initial field of the syllable. But the relation is nonimplicational; we find *l* without *b* (*land*), and we find *b* without *l* (*band*). As a rule, we also find such a nonimplicational relation so long as we are considering only some particular consonant in its relation with some particular vowel. There is a relation between *b* and *e* in the syllable *be*, but the relation is nonimplicational: we can have a syllable with *b* and without *e* (*by*) and a syllable with *e* and without *b* (*me*). It turns out, however—after we have established the categories on the basis of the textual analysis—that there will be an implicational relation between the category of vowels and the category of consonants within the syllable: we cannot have a representative from the category of consonants without having a representative from the category of vowels in the same syllable (cf. p. 35). In the same way, there is nonimplicational relation between a particular subordinate clause and a particular main clause, since the subordinate clause can be replaced by another subordinate clause and the main clause by another main clause; but there is an implicational relation between the category of subordinate clauses and the category of main clauses. It is possible, however, to find implicational relations between particular elements, and, as we shall see shortly, there are many examples to be found of these, both in everyday life and in the world of language.

Implicational relations may be further classified as *reciprocal* or *unilateral*. There is a reciprocal implicational relation between two entities when each presupposes the other; when one presupposes the other, but not vice versa, the relation is unilateral. Examples of *reciprocal implicational relations* are the relations between volume one and volume two of a book, between marriage partners, or between two betrothed—they could not be called what they are unless both existed. Let us add at once: if an author writes a book and calls it volume one, he has, by calling it that, presupposed the existence of volume two, even if that volume never comes out. In the same way, if a man is called a husband, the existence of his wife is presupposed, even though we might never happen to meet her. In other words, we may be given only one entity together with an implicational relation, and on that basis we can *supply* the relation with another entity —not with any particular concrete entity that we could describe in detail, but with an entity about which we know only that it is something presupposed by the first. In such a case, where a presupposed entity is not manifested to us but can be supplied, we say that it is *latent*.

If a language is so constructed as to have no syllables containing a vowel alone, but only syllables containing both vowel and consonant, we say that there is a reciprocal implicational relation between the category of consonants and the category of vowels in the language. But if the syllables of a language may consist of vowel alone or of vowel and consonant, we conclude that the language displays a *unilateral implicational relation* between the category of consonants and the category of vowels: consonant *implies* vowel, but not vice versa; vowel *is implied* by consonant, but not vice versa. Unilateral implicational relation is the usual relation between the category of subordinate clauses and the category of main clauses: subordinate clause implies main clause, but not vice versa; main clause is implied by subordinate clause, but not vice versa. And if we encounter a subordinate clause all by itself without any trace of its main clause, we conclude that the main clause is latent and supply it as needed—not a particular concrete main clause, but one about which we know only that it is a main clause implied by the given subordinate clause. An exclamation like *If I had money*! requires such a supplementation. Examples of unilateral implicational relations are, of course, easy to find outside language as well. In chess, the king is implied by all the other pieces—if the king is mated, all his men are captured and the game is over—but not vice versa.

To be certain of securing an exhaustive description of a language, such that all relations are registered, we cannot straight away break up the text into the smallest elements having demonstrable relation, but must subject the text to a series of successive divisions such that at each step there will be as few parts as possible. In this way, any linguistic text can first be divided into two parts, a *content plane* and an *expression plane*, with reciprocal implicational relation: if it really is a language that we are dealing with, it must have both a content and an expression. Each of these is then further divided into parts and into parts of parts—chapters, paragraphs, sentences, clauses, etc.—down to the smallest elements.

At each step of this division we can set up categories defined by one or another of the relations we have been discussing. One category—for example, that of subordinate clauses or that of consonants—will be defined as implying; another—for example, the category of main clauses or that of vowels—will be defined as implied; and so on. Now an interesting fact is that the members of each such category have the peculiar property that the substitution of one member for another can entail a difference in the opposite plane of the language. The expression elements, for example, that are members of the consonant and vowel categories will each be defined as differing from the other members of the same category by the fact that substitution of any of these others for it can entail a difference in the linguistic content (in the meaning of a sign). The fact that *p, s, r,* and *t* are four different expression elements in English and that *a, e, i,* and *o* are four different expression elements in English can be seen at once from the fact that the exchange of one for another at the same place in the chain entails a difference in the content: *pat, sat, rat, tat, pat, pet, pit, pot* (cf. p. 33). It is with the help of such a *commutation test* that we are able to determine the number of members in a linguistic category. The same, obviously, holds true of the content elements of language: 'nominative' and 'genitive', 'present' and 'preterite', as well as all lexical components, are linguistically different by virtue of the fact that exchanging one for another can entail a difference in the expression. And it is also obvious that this test is applicable not only to what we have here called expression elements and content elements, but to all members whatsoever of all categories whatsoever. For example, two sentences are different only if their contents are different and their expressions are different. If we merely change the expression of a sentence, in such a way as to involve no difference in its content, we have produced only a difference in pronunciation, not a linguistic difference; and if we merely change the content of a sentence, in such a way as to involve no difference in its expression, we have produced only a difference in thought, not a linguistic difference.

We have here arrived at a fundamental property of language, one by which it is distinguished from other structures. Taking the word *commutation* in the special sense in which we have used it, we can give a concise definition of *language* as *a structure in which the members of each category have mutual commutation.*

Clearly, this definition is a very broad one; and when we apply it we must be prepared to discover that it is satisfied by many structures that we are perhaps not accustomed to calling languages, at least not ordinary everyday languages. So, for example, it will turn out that everything we call uniforms, in the broadest sense, including folk costumes and the like, will constitute systems that fit this definition. Every uniform has a corresponding content: this uniform "means" a French officer of a certain rank; this vestment "means" a Roman Catholic prelate of a certain rank; and when, as very often happens, there are different folk costumes for young girls and for married women, each of these "uniforms" likewise has its special "meaning." And the commutation test can be applied here as well: different content corresponds to different expression (different costume), and vice versa. And there will be a number of other areas where we shall find structures proving to be, on this decisive point of commutation, identical with the structures that we are used to calling languages. In so far as they attempt to communicate a content, the various art genres, like descriptive painting, program music, and so on, must be languages in the sense of our definition. A game, if interpreted, will also be a language in this sense—as, for example, a game of chess if it is interpreted as two battle arrays, each consisting of higher and lower ranking officers and privates and, among the higher ranking officers, of king and queen, and so on. In such a case we have both content and expression and can apply the commutation test.

At the same time, we can appropriately narrow our definition somewhat by adding a qualification. If we look at our everyday languages, we shall always find in their structure the peculiar feature that a single expression element does not, as a rule, correspond to (i.e. does not have relation with) a single content element, and vice versa. As we have seen earlier (p. 32), it *may* happen that one expression element will correspond to one content element (e.g. Eng. -*s* as expression of 'genitive'), but this is a special case and is never true of the whole structure of a language. As a rule, a sign consists of two or more expression elements and two or more content elements connected with them. Now as far as the linguistic expression is concerned, we are so fortunate as to know—or to imagine that we know—how many expression elements enter into a given sign. As far as the linguistic content is concerned, at the present stage of research we still lack sufficient information. But we can easily perform a provisional analysis that will be adequate to our present purpose. The expressions of the written English words *ram* and *ewe* can be analyzed into three elements each: the letters *r*, *a*, and *m*, and *e*, *w*, and *e*. As for the content, each word can be analyzed into two elements: 'he-sheep' and 'she-sheep' respectively. We could certainly carry the analysis further by similarly analyzing the word *sheep* (and perhaps also the words *he* and *she*) into components, but that would take us too far for our present purpose. As can already be seen, what we are doing in this content analysis of *ram* and *ewe* is replacing the simple sign-content with a compound content whose components enter into other sign-contents in the language. (Thus, the components 'he' and 'she' enter into the content of the signs *he* and *she*, *boy* and *girl*, *stallion* and *mare*. To what extent the component 'sheep' enters into any compound sign-contents we shall not here inquire, since the answer would require the analysis of 'sheep' that we have deliberately not attempted; at any rate, the component 'sheep' obviously enters into the sign-content of the word *sheep*.) This replacement of a simple sign-content by a compound does not involve any change in the expression: it is all the same whether we say that *ram* means 'ram' or that it means 'he-sheep'. What we have done here with the content corresponds completely to what we are better used to doing with the expression. When we resolve *ram* into *r*, *a*, and *m*, we are replacing the simple (i.e. still unanalyzed) sign-expression with a compound consisting of components that enter into other sign-expressions of the language. Again, this replacement of a simple sign-expression by a compound does not involve any change in the content: it is all the same whether we say that the concept 'ram' is expressed in English by *ram* or by *r*, *a*, and *m*. In both instances, in the content as well as in the expression, we *define* the unanalyzed entity by assembling other entities taken from the same language. This is always the way a definition is made, and the definitions of meaning that are found in dictionaries are to be understood as attempts at the kind of content analysis we have outlined. To avoid misunderstanding, we must also observe that a definition obviously does not consist of a helter-skelter enumeration of the sign components, but posits a special kind of relation between them. The expression definition of *ram* must include the information that *r*, *a*, and *m* appear in just that order, and, correspondingly, the content definition posits a certain logical relation between the components into which the sign-content is analyzed.

Thus, language is not constructed so that each content element will have one and only one corresponding expression element and vice versa, but so that a unit of content elements will correspond to a unit of expression elements and vice versa. The situation is not

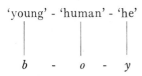

but

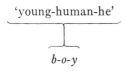

Now we might take this peculiar property into account in our definition of language by adding the following restriction: *If a structure with reciprocal implicational relation between content and expression is to be recognized as a language, we require that there must not be a one-one reciprocal implicational relation throughout between its expression elements and its content elements.*

If we add this restriction, there is no doubt that some of the examples given earlier will no longer qualify as languages. This is a matter of minor importance, and we shall not pursue it further. But the restriction is useful for another reason: outside the domain of everyday languages we are often faced with the difficulty of deciding whether it is necessary to divide a given structure into a content plane and an expression plane; now such a division must be omitted if element corresponds to element between the two planes in such a way that within each plane the elements are defined by precisely the same relations.

Whether or not we add this restriction, we must be prepared to find that various other structures besides everyday languages will qualify as languages according to our definition. An everyday language, then, like Danish, English, or French, is a special kind of language: *By an everyday language is meant a language into which all other languages can be translated.* Every game of chess can be translated into—formulated in—an everyday language, but not vice versa. In general, an everyday language differs from all other kinds of languages (e.g. the mathematician's symbolic language or the chemist's language of formulæ) by not being made especially for particular purposes but being of use for all purposes. In an everyday language we can—with the help of circumlocutions, if necessary, or carefully prepared explanations—formulate anything whatsoever. Any piece of program music, even, will be translatable into a piece of everyday language—but not vice versa. In everyday language, as Søren Kierkegaard has said, one can "work over the inexpressible until it is expressed." This is the advantage of everyday language, and its mystery. And this is why the Polish logician Tarski (who reached the same conclusion independently of the present author) rightly says that everyday languages are characterized in contrast to other languages by their "universalism."

To establish a general theory of linguistic structure, we must start with some definition of language of the kind we have been considering, because the establishment of such a theory is not simply, or even principally, a matter of experience, but rather of calculation. Experience is no adequate basis for a theory of linguistic structure: it would be impossible to go through all existing linguistic texts, and, moreover, it would be futile, since the theory must be valid not only for the texts that have been written or spoken up to now, but also for those that will be written or spoken in the future—that is to say, for all theoretically possible texts and all theoretically possible languages. On the basis of certain experiences, which must necessarily be limited even if they should be as varied as possible, we make a calculation of all conceivable possibilities within certain frames. These frames we set arbitrarily, by taking—as we have just now done—certain features that are present in all the objects commonly called languages and generalizing so as to say: all objects displaying these features I shall call languages. It may turn out that some of the objects falling within the definition are not commonly called languages, but that makes no difference provided only that no objects are excluded that *are* commonly called languages. After we have thus defined— arbitrarily, but appropriately—what we shall understand by a language, we next set up a general calculus for all the objects that will prove to satisfy our definition, a calculus providing for all conceivable cases. This calculus is derived from our definition and in itself is founded, not on experience, but only on reasoning. We need not worry whether the calculus will fit given languages or given texts. The theory of linguistic structure must be so established as to have consistency and exhaustiveness of description built into the calculation, and this requirement cannot be checked by seeing whether the theory really applies to all existing objects (such a check would be impracticable, both because of the number and size of the objects and because the theory must be applicable also to objects that do not yet exist), but only by reexamining the theoretical calculus to see whether it itself is consistent and exhaustive. In this matter the linguistic theoretician behaves like any other theoretician—like a mathematician, for example, who sets up his theory without regard to practical applications but whose theory, for precisely that reason, may be applied to cases that were not foreseen when it was established. An engineer can build a bridge simply by keeping to the mathematician's formulæ. Provided the mathematician's theory is consistent and exhaustive, and the engineer knows it sufficiently well and applies it appropriately, the bridge will hold.

A work of calculation such as we have here programmed in outline is obviously very comprehensive and very difficult. No such work was ever undertaken by classical linguistics, which did not even see the possibility of it. Much effort has since been put into the task, and many attempts have been made to carry it out, but it is still a long way to the establishment of a typology in which the known everyday languages would be distributed and on the basis of which general empirical propositions could be asserted about the structure of everyday language and its internal functions. For that reason, whatever we have to say about these matters must bear a provisional stamp.

We may take it as given that every language has two, and only two, planes: the content plane and the expression plane. In the theory we must also reckon with the possibility that a language may turn out, at the first stage of the analysis, to have three or more planes, but it would be absurd to suppose that such a structure is found in any everyday language and we can therefore ignore the possibility in our present discussion. Each of the two planes, as we have seen, can be divided further and further, down to the minimal entities, which in this book we have called *elements*—content elements and expression elements.

These elements are ordered in *categories*, and a linguistic typology must show what categories can appear in a language, what categories can appear together, permitting or implying one another's presence, and what categories cannot appear together, avoiding one another or implying one another's absence. Just as, within the chain, we distinguished between reciprocal or unilateral implicational relations and nonimplicational relations, so here we can distinguish between *reciprocal* or *unilateral implicational correlations* and *nonimplicational correlations*.

Within each of the two planes of a language, the most comprehensive categories into which the elements fall are those that we shall here call categories of *basic* and *characterizing elements*. This division rests on the special kind of relation that we call *government*. Now, not every kind of government will come into consideration here, but only what we shall call *direction*—the kind of government that serves to establish a clause or a unit composed of clauses. In the clause *sa première femme aimait les fleurs* there is an example of government in the fact that *sa* and *première* are feminine (in contrast to masculine *son* and *premier*) because *femme* is feminine and requires gender agreement of its adjectives; but in this instance the government is not a direction since it does not establish a clause, but only part of a clause (such a part—in our example, *sa première femme*—is called a junction). On the other hand, in the clause *sa première femme était jolie* the government connecting the feminine noun *femme* and the feminine form *jolie* is a direction since by means of it (and of other similar governments) the clause is established as a formal linguistic unit.

Now by a *characterizing element* we shall understand either an element that can enter as governed into a direction or an element entering into paradigm with such an element, while a *basic element* will be an element having neither of these properties. In the content plane of language, the characterizing elements are the *flexional elements* (e.g. 'feminine' in the examples given above), and the basic elements are the *stem elements* (e.g.

the elements that enter into lexical words like 'ram' and 'ewe'). In the expression plane, the characterizing elements are *accents* and *modulations*. In Danish there are two accents, one manifested in pronunciation by a (relatively) strong stress and the other by a (relatively) weak stress. The two have mutual commutation (*kórset* 'the cross' and *korsét* 'corset', whose expressions differ only in accent, have different contents), and they have unilateral implicational relation: the presence of a (relatively) weak stress in an utterance presupposes the presence of a (relatively) strong stress, but not vice versa. Moreover, this implicational relation is a direction, sufficient in itself to establish an expression clause. In standard Danish there are also two modulations. One, manifested in pronunciation by a falling tone, is found in apodoses and concluding clauses; the other, manifested in pronunciation by a non-falling tone, is found in conditional and introductory clauses and serves in general to give notice that the utterance is not finished and that more is to be expected (and if that "more" does not appear, the modulation permits us to supply it). As is already clear from what has been said, these two modulations have a unilateral implicational relation: the presence of a non-falling tone in an utterance presupposes the presence of a falling tone, but not vice versa. Moreover, this implicational relation is a direction, sufficient in itself to establish a unit of expression clauses.

Provisional results indicate that every language has in its content plane both flexional elements (in our sense of the term) and stem elements; even the so-called isolating languages have certain "particles" that enter as governed elements into direction. The expression plane, however, does not always display the corresponding distinction between accent and modulation on the one hand and basic elements on the other. In ordinary written Danish we have neither accent nor modulation in the usual sense. To be sure, we have punctuation marks, like the question mark, which "points ahead" to a following answer (which may, if required, be supplied), but such punctuation marks are not an absolute necessity. Many languages lack accents in pronunciation. French is an example. To be sure, it is possible to interchange stronger and weaker stress in pronouncing French, but it is never possible to distinguish the content of two words by a different distribution of stress as in Danish *kórset—korsét*. Whether all languages have modulations is an open question, if only because classical descriptions of languages generally give no account of modulations.

Thus we can expect to find in the system of human language (so far as concerns everyday language, to which we are here restricting our discussion) a unilateral implicational correlation—in the expression plane, at any rate—between characterizing elements and basic elements: a language cannot have accent and modulation without having basic elements of expression (e.g. vowels and consonants), but it can have the latter without the former. In the content plane there may perhaps be a reciprocal implicational correlation between flexional elements and stem elements.

These two main categories, or *species*, of elements—characterizing and basic—can be further divided into *types*. It would be too complicated to explain here how this division into types is actually effected according to the theory, but in practice we can say that we divide the characterizing elements into those that can be used to characterize a whole utterance or such as enter into paradigm with these and, on the other hand, those that lack this property. The former are called *extense*, and the latter *intense*. In the expression plane, the modulations are the extense elements and the accents are the intense elements. In the content plane, the extense elements are those that are commonly called elements of verbal inflexion (tense and mood, for example), while the intense elements are those that are commonly called elements of nominal inflexion (case and number, for example). The basic elements are divided into *central*—those that are indispensable in a minimal unit, or such as enter into paradigm with these—and *peripheral*—those that are dispensable in a minimal unit. In the expression plane, where the minimal unit involved is the syllable, the indispensable elements are the *vowels* and the dispensable elements are the *consonants*. In the content plane we find corresponding "content syllables" (they can be called minimal syntagmata and in practice will often coincide with individual words), divisible into indispensable or *radical elements* (e.g. the elements that enter into 'faith' in the relation 'un-faith-ful') and *derivational elements* (e.g. the elements that enter into 'un-' and '-ful').

After what has been said above, we can reckon with the possibility of a language's having modulations without having accents (French, for example), but hardly the other way round. Thus we have here a unilateral implicational correlation. It is a fact that a language cannot have consonants without also having vowels, but this is simply a consequence of the way we have defined vowel and consonant. Instead of vowels and consonants, a language may have a third, undifferentiated category of expression elements. Thus, there are languages with "vowel harmony" (e.g. Finnish, Hungarian, and Turkish), in which one vocoid (vocalic sound) in a chain determines the choice of all the other vocoids in the chain. In such languages, then, the vocoids represent accents, since they can enter as governed elements into a direction. And from this it follows that the contoids (consonantal sounds) do not represent consonants in such languages, but rather an undifferentiated category of expression elements. As for the content plane, it seems to be true that a language can have verbal, without having nominal, flexional elements (this is probably the case with the true isolating type of language, like Classical Chinese), but perhaps not the other way round. And apparently a language can have radical, without having derivational, elements, but certainly not the other way round. Here, then, there seems to be a unilateral implicational correlation.

The types, in turn, can be further divided into *subtypes* according to their implicational relations. As for the basic elements, the central type can be divided into those that must necessarily be present in the central part of the syllable (or syntagma) and those that need not be. Correspondingly, the peripheral type can be divided into those that must necessarily be present in the peripheral part and those that need not be. In the expression plane, for example, consonants can be so divided into two categories, one of which is represented by sounds or letters that stand at the beginning of the syllable, the other by those that stand at the end—or one category may be represented by those that occupy the first place in a group, the other by those that occupy the second place. The division of the flexional elements into subtypes is particularly important. They may be divided into elements that can establish a compound sentence (or elements entering into paradigm with these) and elements that cannot. Case, for example, can serve only to establish a single clause: case direction never extends over the boundary of the single clause. Other flexional categories, however, do admit direction extending over the clause boundary: in *les fleurs sont jolies, et elles sont fraîches* a direction between feminine plural forms is to be found in each of the two clauses; but the feminine plural *elles* in the second clause is chosen because of a feminine plural in the preceding clause, which it presupposes, and there thus arises still another feminine plural direction binding the two clauses together into a compound sentence. This illustrates the way in which the various "grammatical categories" (case, gender, tense, mood, etc.) are defined in the linguistic structure.

The division into subtypes seems not to be universal in languages, but it is very common so far as flexional elements are concerned. With the help of the commutation test we can discover how many elements are found in each of the categories in a given language and what numerical relationships govern the structure of human language in general in this respect. Characteristically, the number of the elements is always relatively small. After all, the possibility of forming a practically un-limited number of signs with a small number of elements is implied in the very essence and purpose of language. But within the individual categories that happen to be represented in any given language, the number varies quite considerably. There are languages with two vowels and languages with twelve, or perhaps more, and all the numbers in between. There are generally more consonants than vowels. The number of accents and modulations seems always to be quite small, while in the content plane the number of flexional elements may be relatively small, as in English or Danish, or quite large. There are languages with two cases and languages with over fifty. There are languages with two numbers (singular and plural), with three (like Lithuanian or Ancient Greek, which also have a dual), and with four or five (like certain languages of the Pacific, with their trial and quadral numbers). There are languages with two genders (like French and Danish, if we leave the pronoun out of account), with three (German), with four (as in the Danish pronoun *han* 'he', *hun* 'she', *den* 'it [common gender]', *det* 'it [neuter gender]'), and with as many as sixteen (Bantu). The least developed categories within the flexional system seem to be person, comparison, and verbal mood (English has two moods: indicative *lives*, imperative-subjunctive-infinitive *live*; Danish has three: indicative *lever*, imperative *lev*, subjunctive-infinitive *leve*; German and Latin, in contrast to English and Danish, distinguish between the subjunctive and the infinitive, and Greek adds to these a separate optative).

This little survey is, of course, both incomplete and provisional, intended merely to suggest the first results that we might hope to obtain from a typology of linguistic structure. What we are eventually to gain from it—and what could not be shown in these examples—is the establishment of general laws stating what categories a language *can* have, what categories it *must* have, and what categories are bound together in a general implicational relationship.

In analyzing a language, we must add to the registration of the elements a registration of their *variants*. Two kinds of variants are to be found: the *varieties*, which are bound to their environments in a reciprocal implicational relation, and the *variations*, which vary freely and have only nonimplicational relation with their environments. The significance of this distinction can perhaps be seen most easily if we consider the representation of the expression elements in handwriting. A letter may take on different shapes depending on the other letters it is connected with: these are varieties. But each variety may in turn take on different shapes each time it is written: these are variations. Correspondingly, as shown by physical analysis, there are varieties and variations of spoken sounds. From the point of view of linguistic structure this division into variants is universal, i.e. it can be performed by an advance calculation on any entities whatsoever: any entity has as many varieties as it has possibilities of relation, and each of these varieties can be further divided into as many as an infinite number of variations. The peculiar fact is that the division into varieties and the division into variations are exhausted by turns: in a continued analysis there first comes a point at which varieties can no longer be divided into varieties, but only into variations; then comes a point at which variations can no longer be divided into variations, but only into varieties, and so on. We can see this most easily by considering variants of content entities. If we take the content of a sign like the word *man*, we can divide it into varieties until, for example, we reach the category of the men who can stand in the place where I am now standing, and at that point we cannot make any further division into varieties. But we can divide these varieties further into variations, namely, the different men who can stand in this place. These cannot be further divided into variations, but they can be divided into varieties—into each of these men in different places. These can be divided into variations—into each of these men in each of these places at different points of time. These can be divided into varieties—as seen from different points of view. And these, again, can be divided into variations—as seen by different people. A variation that cannot be divided into variations, but only into varieties, we call an *individual*. A variety that cannot be divided into varieties, but only into variations, we call a *localized* variety. As is evident from the example, there are individuals and localized varieties of different degrees.

# Types of Linguistic Usage

Classical linguistics particularly cultivated the study of sounds (*phonology, phonetics*) from both physiological and physical points of view, and one might expect that a *phonetic* typology of languages could be set up as part of a typology of linguistic usage for the expression plane of language. Its aim would be to establish that certain linguistic communities use certain sounds while certain other linguistic communities use certain other sounds to represent the expression elements of their languages. And of course, in view of what we have said earlier, it would be concerned not merely with individual sounds, but with classes of sounds, sound *categories*.

In fact, classical phonetics has categorized speech sounds from many different points of view. It has divided them into sounds pronounced with more open mouth—what we shall call *vocoids*—and sounds produced with more closed mouth—the *contoids*. Both these main categories can be further divided in many ways: for example, according to the movements of the speech organs used to produce them, and according to the place where the movements occur. In this way the vocoids have been divided, for example, into open and close, front and back, rounded (i.e. pronounced with rounding of the lips) and unrounded, nasal and non-nasal. Similarly, the contoids have been divided into such categories as labials, dentals, and velars; stops, fricatives, and affricates; nasals and non-nasals; voiced and voiceless; and so on.

Against such divisions, the linguistically legitimate objection has been made that such categories can never have any fixed boundaries, whether from the physical (physiological) or from the linguistic point of view. From the physical (physiological) point of view, only continuous transitions are found between such categories. Between open and close sounds any number of half-open or half-close can be added. Between front and back vocoids can be found central vocoids and all sorts of other nuances. A sound can be strongly or weakly, wholly or partly, nasalized, voiced, or rounded, and so on. Neither from the linguistic point of view are there any universally fixed boundaries, if we compare the expression elements of different languages and their usual phonetic representations. When we apply the commutation test to the expression elements in different languages, it becomes evident that there is no fixed relationship between the boundaries laid down in the phonetic sphere by the categories of a linguistic structure and the boundaries that can be established between the *phonetic* categories from a physical or physiological point of view. There is no simple coincidence between the vowel and consonant categories and the physiologically defined categories of vocoids and contoids. In the Czech words *vlk* and *krk* (p. 38), *l* and *r* are vowels, but at the same time contoids (cf. also Eng. *little*). In the interjections of many languages, various contoids may be vowels (cf. *pst, hm*). Conversely, vocoids may be consonants (as, very frequently, *i* and *u*, which are then often represented orthographically by *y* and *w*). Since each language lays down its own boundaries, languages are not congruent from a phonetic point of view, and this will hold true as long as one continues the analysis. Because the number of expression elements differs from language to language, there clearly can be no fixed relationship between them and the sound categories that represent them. In French and English, voiced and voiceless *s* represent two different expression elements, as shown by the commutation test (Fr. *poison* 'poison' and *poisson* 'fish' differ in expression only in having voiced and voiceless *s* respectively; so also Eng. *zeal* and *seal*), but Danish makes no such distinction. In Danish, voiced *s* could be substituted anywhere for the customary voiceless *s* without any risk of confusion or misunderstanding, while that would be impossible in French or English. In French and Finnish, *t* and *d* are principally distinguished in pronunciation by the fact that *t* is unvoiced and *d* is voiced. In Danish, the principal distinction is that *t* is aspirated (followed by an *h*-sound) while *d* is not. Here again, different boundaries have been laid down within the phonetic sphere by the different languages, so that a Frenchman will take a Danish *d* for a *t*, and a Dane, unless he has special training, will be incapable of hearing any difference between *d* and *t* in French or in Finnish. On the other hand, no confusion or misunderstanding can possibly arise in French or in Finnish if an aspirated *t* is substituted for the unaspirated *t* that is usual in those languages, or in Danish if a voiced *d* is substituted for the usual voiceless *d*. Finnish makes no distinction between *k* and *g*, or between *p* and *b*; in both writing and pronunciation, only *k* and *p* are usually found. As a consequence, a Finn will be unable without special training to grasp the distinction that other languages make in this respect; and, on the other hand, it will be possible to substitute Dan. *g* and *b* or Fr. *g* and *b* for the usual Finn. *k* and *p* in any Finnish word without danger of confusion or misunderstanding. These are only individual examples; the situation is the same everywhere—the phonetic systems of languages are incongruent, and for that reason it is impossible to establish a universal phonetic system having any linguistic validity.

One might think to achieve better results by starting from some other matching of linguistic structure and linguistic usage than the one we have chosen. We have assumed that all conceivable (physically possible) sounds might represent, or be made to represent, variants of a language's expression elements, even such sounds as are not customarily or deliberately used in the language under consideration. We have said, for example, that we *could* introduce a voiced *s* in Danish, or that in Finnish we *could* introduce an aspirated *t* instead of the unaspirated *t*, or *g* and *b* instead of *k* and *p*. It may be objected that while theoretically we could do this, in fact we do not. Danish *s*, when pronounced correctly, is *always* voiceless, Finnish *t* is *always* unaspirated, and Finnish *k* and *p* are *always* *k* and *p*, never *g* and *b*. This apparently very plausible objection, however, actually involves an extraordinarily rash assumption. How can we know these things? It is certainly impossible to examine everything that everybody has ever said in Danish or in Finnish, let alone what nobody has yet said but what will be said in those languages. For this reason, linguists in general wisely refrain from asserting that something *cannot be pronounced* in some particular way in a given language. Rather, they are content with saying in what ways (*among others*, understood) it *can* be pronounced. And yet there seems to be something tempting in the thought that within the whole continuum of possible sounds of human speech there might, in each linguistic usage, be certain no-man's-lands, zones unoccupied by any linguistic expression element. If so, it would not only be true that each language lays down its own boundaries in the phonetic domain, but it would also be true that each language selects its own areas therein. Thus, we might imagine a linguistic usage containing back and front vocoids, but no central vocoids, or unrounded vocoids, but no rounded ones. But whenever we undertake to investigate a linguistic usage in any considerable detail, we find ourselves disappointed in such expectations, and the thesis can hardly be maintained in so sharp a formulation.

We might perhaps try something else: following the English phonetician Daniel Jones, we might divide the sounds that appear as variants of a single speech sound (a single phoneme—i.e. a single phonetic representative of an expression element) into principal variants and secondary variants. In languages where front and back, but not central, vocoids are sounds of common occurrence, we could say that the different possible nuances of front and back vocoids were principal variants of their respective speech sounds (phonemes) while the central vocoids were subsidiary variants. Similarly, in languages (like

English or Russian) in which unrounded front vocoids occur commonly, but rounded ones only in special cases, we could say that the former are principal variants, and the latter subsidiary variants, of their respective speech sounds (phonemes). But the very difficult question here is how one is to eliminate arbitrariness and subjectivity from these decisions: whether something is "of common occurrence" or "frequent" is a matter of opinion.

It is unlikely, therefore, that we can construct a phonetic typology otherwise than by indicating what boundaries the linguistic structure can lay down in the phonetic domain. It is at least doubtful that we could declare certain zones to be no-man's-lands within a given language and thus arrive at tenable general propositions about an implicational correlation between phonetic categories. An extraordinarily fascinating attempt in this direction has been made by the Russian-Czech linguist Roman Jakobson (now in the United States), who thinks it possible to show that children the world over learn the speech sounds in a fixed order—first certain sounds and then others—and that the child's building up of the phonetic system of his language will be reversed if the faculty of speech is lost in aphasia resulting from a brain lesion, when the phonetic system will be broken down by the victim's forgetting first the sounds that the child acquires last, and last the sounds that the child acquires first. Finally—and here we come to the decisive point —it is claimed that the resulting phonetic hierarchy will be reflected in the phonetic systems of linguistic usage, so that certain languages will have only the sounds that the child learns first and the aphasic forgets last, others will have, in addition, the sounds that the child learns next, and so on. With respect to children's language and speech disturbances, advance theoretical objections can hardly be made against the hypothesis (but since it is derived solely from observation it must be either confirmed or invalidated by further observation, and it is impossible to predict what the outcome will be); in so far, however, as it is transferred to the study of the structure of phonetic systems, theoretical misgivings arise from the fact that it presupposes the existence of a phonetic no-man's-land in a linguistic usage. Part of it can, in all likelihood, be maintained, even in respect of linguistic sound systems, namely the part involving an implicational relationship, not between sounds, but between linguistically determined phonetic boundaries. For example, although it probably could not be maintained that the existence of velar contoids in a language presupposes the existence of labial and dental contoids, it might possibly be maintained that the existence of, say, a linguistic boundary (i.e. a boundary separating representatives of two different expression elements) between front and back close rounded vowels (cf. Fr. *lu* and *loup*) presupposes the existence of a linguistic boundary between front and back half-close rounded vowels (cf. Fr. *feu* and *faux*). But this hypothesis, too, is based solely on observation and must therefore be confirmed or invalidated by observation; and here, too, predicting the outcome is risky.

In the study of meaning (*semantics*) we should expect to be able to arrive at a typology of linguistic usage for the content plane of language. This is for many reasons a more difficult task than phonetic typology, partly because semantics has been much less cultivated and partly because it embraces a far greater domain. The content of language is nothing less than the world surrounding us, and the minimal particular meanings of a word, the particular meanings that are individuals (cf. p. 114) are the *things* of the world: the lamp that stands here on my desk is a particular meaning of the word *lamp*; I myself am a particular meaning of the word *man*. But these *things* naturally organize themselves into many kinds of *categories*, and another difficulty is that one hardly knows what sort of a science is concerned with the establishment of these categories. With a certain justice one could say that it is all the sciences taken together. All sciences other than linguistics are actually theories of the linguistic content studied independently of the linguistic structure, just as physiological phonetics and physical acoustics are the study of the linguistic expression independently of the linguistic structure. In particular, we might think of psychology as being the science, if there is one, that could furnish such a categorization of experienced things as would be suitable for mapping on the system of categories furnished by the linguistic structure. It is to be hoped that recent attempts of psychologists at a "phenomenological" description of the outside world as it is immediately experienced may lead to a fruitful collaboration with linguistics. It behooves us to maintain a more skeptical attitude toward the attempts—especially favored in former times—to found a linguistic semantics on the logic of ideas. For one thing, such an attempt runs in a vicious circle: conceptual logic is based on language (Aristotle's logic, for example, would never have come to have the shape it has if it had not been thought in Greek); conceptual logic is always a language in disguise, and transforming or refining it seems to make no difference.

The prospects for a typology of meaning are therefore still poor. And we must realize in advance that it will face the same difficulties as the typology of sounds. Each language draws its own boundaries in the world of things and ideas. A sign in one language does not correspond to a sign in another language, as every translator knows. From the point of view of the world of things, just as of the world of sounds, there is no congruence between languages. And whether we can rightly find within the world of things or ideas certain zones that are subsidiary variants or no-man's-lands in given languages is highly doubtful. Here, as in respect of phonetic typology, it will at best be a matter of establishing implicational relationships, not between meanings, but between linguistically determined boundaries of meaning.

As the preceding considerations indicate, a typology of linguistic usage has crucial difficulties to contend with. The only kind of linguistic typology that seems realizable on an objective basis is, paradoxically enough, the one that classical linguistics never suspected to be possible: the typology of linguistic structure.

# Linguistic Change

The great discovery that resulted from nineteenth-century research in genetic linguistics and that came to put its stamp on most of the linguistics of that period is that *languages change*. The different members of a language family may be considered as so many transformations of their common origin, the parent language, and in the history of the individual languages continual changes can also be observed and different stages can be distinguished. Because of the one-sided interest that classical linguistics had in usage, at the expense of structure, it was easy to exaggerate the importance of this discovery. For it is obvious that while linguistic structure is something relatively stable, which may well change in the course of time but which often remains constant over very long periods, linguistic usage is far more changeable. Words and other signs are ceaselessly arising and passing into obsolescence; pronunciations and meanings vary from place to place and shift from decade to decade, and indeed, under a more profound analysis, display a constant drift. For a science that saw nothing in language except signs, their pronunciations, and their meanings —and which, moreover, had celebrated its great triumphs in discoveries about linguistic change—this was bound to lead with almost fatal necessity to the abandonment of the concept of *linguistic state* (*état de langue*).

Meanwhile, sooner or later, this one-sided attitude was bound to come up against difficulties, and the very doctrine of language families and language change, when carried through, was to lead to a new and deeper understanding of the linguistic state. For it is clear that the parent language itself, known only as a set of formulæ designating the element-functions, is in itself a linguistic state and, what is more, a linguistic state in which all that is given is the linguistic structure. Even if we wished to go so far as not to admit any connexion between our Indo-European formulæ and any reality beyond the element-functions alone, it cannot be denied that when the formulæ are gathered together, as above on pp. 26–27, they constitute something which appears in all respects as the expression system of a language, a system of expression elements. To be sure, our formulæ —alias elements of the parent language—are each defined only as representing a certain function of elements between the genetically related languages. But we simply cannot avoid defining them by their functions *with one another* as well, ordering them in categories just like the expression elements of any other language, and dividing them into vowels, coefficients, consonants, accents, and so on. Moreover, it has proved to be not only unavoidable, but also highly fruitful, to establish rules governing the possible combinations of vowels and coefficients in diphthongs, as well as a whole set of rules concerning word formation which are not merely—or essentially—concerned with the expression elements of the linguistic state involved, but first and foremost with its content elements, or at any rate its content units, and their possible combinations (cf. p. 29). Even if we do not venture to take the whole step of assigning real existence to the totality of our formulæ, and thus equating them with a linguistic state, we still cannot ignore the fact that these formulæ constitute a *system*.

Such a systematic view of the formulæ was first taken by the Swiss linguist Ferdinand de Saussure in a work dated 1879, which was to mark a turning point in the history of linguistics although the point of view that it represented was too strange to his contemporaries for it to meet with any general understanding. Indeed, even if the practical significance of Saussure's discoveries is now recognized by everyone working on genetic problems in Indo-European, it is perhaps only quite recently that we have become fully prepared to understand the theoretical scope of this work. Its distinctive feature is that, on the one hand, it treats the formulæ as a system and draws all the consequences that follow, while on the other hand it does not attribute any other kind of reality to them and thus does not consider them as prehistoric sounds with a certain pronunciation which by gradual change became the sounds of the individual Indo-European languages.

This point of view was bound to lead to practical advances in the elucidation of Indo-European itself. Precisely because Saussure treats the formulæ as a system and, moreover, as a system independent of any concrete phonetic definitions—in short, as a pure linguistic structure—he is led in this work to apply to the Indo-European parent language, the very stronghold of the theory of linguistic change, methods destined to set a pattern in the analysis of any état de langue, methods that can be taken as models of the way in which a linguistic structure should be analyzed. Saussure takes the system in and for itself and puts the question, How do I analyze it so as to obtain the simplest and most elegant explanation? In other words, What is the smallest number of formulæ or elements that I need to account for this entire mechanism?

And at this point Saussure came to do things with the Indo-European system that nobody had been able to do before, and thus to introduce a new method, a structural method into genetic linguistics.

Let us take an example. We have observed above (p. 30) that Indo-European has a vowel alternation $*e : *o : \emptyset$, which appears in diphthongs as $*e\underset{.}{i} : *o\underset{.}{i} : *i, *e\underset{.}{u} : *o\underset{.}{u} : *u$, etc. In addition, one finds in Indo-European a different kind of alternation —or something that might look like a different kind of alternation—namely, a shift between long vowel and $*_A$. This is seen, for example, in

|  |  |  |
|---|---|---|
| OI *sthi-táḥ* 'standing' | : | *ti-ṣṭhā-mi* 'I stand' |
| Lat. *sta-tus* | : | *stā-re* 'to stand' |
| IE root form $*st_A$ | : | $*stā-$ |

or in

| | | |
|---|---|---|
| OI *di-táḥ* 'given' | : | *dá-nam* 'a gift', *dá-dā-mi* 'I give' |
| Lat. *da-tus* | : | *dō-num* |
| IE root form *$d$A- | : | *$d\bar{o}$- |

(We recall that OI *i* = Lat. *a* is IE *A; see p. 17.)

Now Saussure realized that if the long vowel in these alternations were interpreted as a combination of short vowel with *A, the two kinds of alternations, which had before looked entirely different, would become quite the same:

| | | | | | |
|---|---|---|---|---|---|
| | *$e\underset{.}{i}$ | : | *$o\underset{.}{i}$ | : | *$i$ |
| ≠ | *$e\underset{.}{u}$ | : | *$o\underset{.}{u}$ | : | *$u$ |
| ≠ | *$e$A | : | *$o$A | : | *A. |

The row containing *A thus becomes quite parallel with the rows containing *$i$, *$u$, or any other coefficient. All are special cases of the row *$e$ : *$o$ : Ø, and *A is to be taken as a coefficient on a line with *$i$, *$u$, *$r$, *$l$, *$n$, and *$m$. (We may add that it was Saussure who introduced the term "coefficient," and we may note at the same time that Saussure also introduced another term into linguistics, one that has since found high favor with linguists, namely, the term "phoneme" (cf. p. 118). He introduced it, for lack of a better word, as designation for the expression elements of language in order to avoid confusion with the "sounds" of linguistic usage—that is, to designate the purely "algebraic entities" of his theory. By an irony of fate, Saussure's theory was so basically misunderstood by his contemporaries and by many who came after them that the term is now generally used as a synonym for "linguistic sound"— precisely what Saussure was trying to avoid.)

Perhaps this discovery of Saussure's may not seem so very impressive. If so, the reason is that in the foregoing presentation of it the material has been organized for the reader, and thereby the solution has been made fairly obvious. If we consider the commonly held notions of that time, however, the effect must have been quite surprising, if only because, as we have seen (p.

29), the short vowels *e and *o can also alternate with the long vowels *ē and *ō (cf., for example, the Greek nominative *rhḗtōr* 'speaker', with *ō, and the accusative *rhḗtor-a*, with *o) so that the long vowel alternating with *A might be thought to be functionally on a line with the long vowels alternating with zero and not, as it turned out, with the corresponding short vowels.

This reinterpretation of the long vowels alternating with *A as short vowel + *A was possible, of course, only because the combination of short vowel + *A does not appear otherwise in Indo-European; yet it meant a sharp break with the previous method of reconstruction because a formula like Saussure's *oA is founded, not on the element-functions between the Indo-European languages, but on an internal function within the parent language. If the evidence were limited to the element-functions between the Indo-European languages known in Saussure's time, there would be no grounds for distinguishing between the ō in *dō-num* and the ō in *rhḗtōr*. If the ō in *dō-num*, but not the ō in *rhḗtōr*, can be interpreted as *oA, it is not because of a function between different languages, but because of a function between constituents of a single linguistic state. What has happened here is that one algebraic entity has been equated with the product of two others; the operation recalls that of the chemist who analyzes water as a product of hydrogen and oxygen. This kind of operation is required in the analysis of any linguistic state if the simplest possible description is to be achieved. Paradoxically, the first to which this operation was applied in the history of linguistic science was the Indo-European parent language.

In a paper published at the same time as Saussure's and independently of it, the Danish linguist Herman Møller entertained similar ideas and discovered a new and very important simplification as well: the opposition between the three long vowels *ē, *ō, and ā can be interpreted, not as Saussure had interpreted it, by using a single coefficient *A, but by using three. Thus, instead of *ē : *A, *ō : *A, *ā : *A, it is possible to write

$*a_{A_1} : *_{A_1}, *a_{A_2} : *_{A_2}, *a_{A_3} : *_{A_3}$. Later, Møller found that certain short vowels—$*e, *o, *a$—could be explained in analogous fashion as products of the same coefficients and the same vowel: $*e = *_{A_1}a, *o = *_{A_2}a, *a = *_{A_3}a$.

To understand what is essential and important in these reductions from a methodological point of view, we must realize that they constitute a kind of resolution of the Indo-European entities into algebraic or chemical products. This does not proceed directly from comparison of the several Indo-European languages, but from further treatment of the results of such comparison, from an analysis of those results. *Later*, long after the analysis had been made, it was discovered that there is an Indo-European language that distinguishes between $*\bar{o}$ alternating with $*o$ and $*\bar{o}$ alternating with $*_A$, namely Hittite, where the Polish linguist Kuryłowicz was able to show that $h$ sometimes corresponds to IE $*_A$. Moreover, Møller was able to confirm his theory by referring to Hamito-Semitic: that Hamito-Semitic has special consonants corresponding to the different Indo-European coefficients is, in fact, a cornerstone in his demonstration of the genetic relationship between Indo-European and Hamito-Semitic. These confirmations, obtained through consideration of previously unknown element-functions between the genetically related languages, are certainly of the greatest interest, especially in showing that the internal analysis of a linguistic structure like that of the Indo-European parent language bears strong realistic implications. It might be thought that this kind of analysis would lead us astray in a world of abstractions, but quite to the contrary, it puts us on the watch for element-functions remaining to be discovered. Through analysis of the linguistic state we have truly achieved a deeper understanding of the linguistic structure. On the other hand, these confirmations from Hittite and Hamito-Semitic are still merely confirmations, and the internal analysis of the element system of the parent language could be pursued without reference to them.

In the wake of these discoveries of Saussure and Møller concerning the structure of the parent language, various others followed, some made by the same two scholars and some by others. The analytical principle involved, according to which an attempt is made to reduce to a minimum the number of element-formulæ needed for each stage of development of a language—a method that has been followed in the study of all linguistic states since its first application to the Indo-European parent language—has contributed to the introduction of a completely new technique within Indo-European genetic and comparative linguistics. In the chapter on genetic relationship we kept to the classical picture, obtained by mechanical registration of the element-functions between languages, but the system of formulæ that we ended up with (pp. 26–27) has been significantly reduced by this new principle of analysis. It would carry us too far afield, however, to go into details of the extensive reductions that result, interesting as they are. Suffice it to mention that it has been possible to explain combinations of consonant $+ h$ as combinations of consonant $+$ coefficient $*_A$, and to explain the long vowels alternating with $*e$ and $*o$, as well as the zero with which they alternate, and accentual oppositions (circumflex and acute; see p. 21) as varieties conditioned by the location of the word accent and by the number of latent syllables. Analytical reductions of this kind lead to an extraordinarily simple system of Indo-European formulæ.

There is another way, too, in which the linguistic state can be seen to assert itself and claim its rights in the face of an all too one-sided view of linguistic change. The best way to show this, perhaps, is by considering linguistic change itself. If— to use an artificial example for simplicity's sake—we find a language in which $p$ has become $f$ at the beginning of words, but has remained $p$ in other positions, there must have been a period in the history of the language when every word-initial $p$ was mechanically changed to $f$. This would be a *sound law* in the true sense, on a line with any other law prevailing in a society, e.g. a juridical law: from the moment the law came into effect till the moment it ceased to prevail, it was in force and implied the mechanical conversion into *f* of initial *p* in any word coming within the society's range, whether the word was inherited, borrowed, or newly formed. (This is precisely why loan words may deviate in their external shape from inherited words: they have been borrowed after some law has ceased to prevail.) But is such a sound law truly a law of change or a law of state? If a society has a law decreeing that under certain conditions every young man of a certain age shall become a soldier, can it later be said that all such young men became soldiers? Undoubtedly it can, but the change referred to in those terms has its cause in a state of affairs. So long as that state of affairs continues—so long as the law is in force—it would be incorrect to speak of any change. What one can speak of is a mechanical conversion of one element to another under given conditions. So long as the law is in force, every word-initial *p* is mechanically converted to an *f*. This is the same kind of conversion law as the law in chess that a pawn, when it reaches the other side of the board, may have its value converted to that of a queen. The "change" takes place, or may take place, every time we play chess, and it will, or may, take place whether we play chess tomorrow or a year from now. It is not a change: it is a state.

The reader who is not a professional linguist will perhaps be surprised that the author can speak so warmly about so simple a matter. The reason is that only in our times are linguists working themselves free of a one-sided view of change. In fact, much of what has been considered one-sidedly from the point of view of linguistic change is to be seen as static phenomena. We have shown above (p. 16) that a special element-function can be established for IE *\*m* at the end of a word: in that particular position, Greek, for example, has -*n* instead of -*m*. But actually this must not be set up as a distinct element-function. If we first give an account, as we must, of the static laws prevailing in each language, then this special element-function is superfluous. The fact that in Greek "-*m* becomes -*n*" is not an historical change that Greek has undergone, but a rule of the game that holds in the Greek system: in the structure of the Greek language, *m* is an expression element that is partly defined by its inability to stand at the end of the word, and therefore, whenever it would fall in that forbidden position, it must be replaced by -*n*. This is no more wonderful than the fact that we have to convert our money every time we cross the border between two countries. We must do so because each species of coin can be used only in its own place, and this is no law of change. Thus, linguistic change presupposes linguistic state, and thus, genetic linguistics presupposes the theory of linguistic structure, or grammar, which in fact means typological linguistics. Only after we have completely described the linguistic structure in all the individual linguistic states and found a place in them for everything that can be placed there, are we justified in proceeding to compare them from a genetic point of view. In this way, genetic linguistics will be simplified and clarified to an undreamt-of degree.

But even if more weight is thus assigned to linguistic state and less to linguistic change, the fact remains that language does change. And the linguist must seek a causal explanation of this change. This disputed and quite unclarified question is considerably simplified if we hold fast to the distinction between linguistic structure and linguistic usage. There can be many and various reasons for changes in linguistic usage, i.e. for changes in pronunciation (sound laws in the narrower sense), changes in meaning, changes in signs (words). Man is a capricious and enigmatic creature, and here, man is at work. The only provisional statement to be made with any certainty is that the sound changes undergone by a language in the course of time may often be summed up in certain predominant *tendencies* which a given population may stick to for centuries with remarkable tenacity. Maurice Grammont has shown strikingly how such tendencies toward altering pronunciation in certain directions have been at work in the eastern Indo-European languages from the oldest to the most recent times, constantly seizing hold of new material susceptible to change. What lies behind these tendencies is another question. They may be habits of a psychological nature. We encounter such tendencies in everyday life whenever we hear a foreigner speaking our native language. His "speaking with an accent" means precisely that by virtue of his tendencies of pronunciation, his psychological habits, he displaces the sound system of the language in certain directions. These tendencies are acquired, of course, not innate. But the difficulties connected with learning to pronounce a foreign language like a native show that these acquired habits are almost ineradicable, and one can therefore understand how they can be stubbornly maintained from generation to generation over long periods of time.

The reasons for changes in the linguistic structure, on the other hand, cannot lie in tendencies of the speakers. Linguistic structure, after all, is defined as something independent of them. We assume that linguistic structure follows its own laws and that a change in linguistic structure is not due to tendencies of the speakers, but to *dispositions* in the system that undergoes change. A given linguistic structure may be thought of as being predisposed to move in certain directions and not in others. And here it is linguistic typology, with what it has to say about categories that seek out and favor each other and categories that shun or avoid each other, which must identify the causes of linguistic change.

# Languages of
# Different Degrees

Every science aims to provide a procedure by means of which objects of a given nature are to be described. This is always done by introducing a *language* by means of which the objects can be described: a set of terms is introduced—a terminology with accompanying definitions—and then the description is made by using these terms to form sentences concerning the object in question.

Linguistics aims to provide a procedure by means of which languages are to be described. This is done by introducing a language by means of which languages can be described. Such a language for describing languages is called a *metalanguage*, and the language described is called an *object language*. Owing to the universalism of everyday language, an everyday language can be used as metalanguage to describe itself as object language: it is possible, for example, to write a Danish grammar in Danish. In general, however, it will be necessary to change somewhat the linguistic *usage* of the everyday language by introducing a number of new signs, the so-called technical terms. It is also possible to replace the everyday language, wholly or in part, with a specially invented symbolic language suitable for use as a metalanguage to describe other languages. This is also done in linguistics, but we have not used that kind of metalanguage in this book.

Thus we see that there can be languages of different degrees: first-degree languages, and second-degree languages, or metalanguages. Theoretically, of course, we can continue the progression: a language that describes a metalanguage will be a third-degree language, or a second-degree metalanguage (also called a meta-metalanguage). And we shall see that this theoretical possibility is actually found.

The grammar, or description, of the individual état de langue is thus a first-degree metalanguage. Using the terms introduced at various points in the preceding chapters, we can now briefly sum up the procedure of grammar by saying that it starts from a chain or a text as object for analysis, argues from that to a unilateral presupposition between the chain (the text) and the paradigms (the chain presupposes the paradigms), and, finally, on that basis, supplies the paradigms.

Like all sciences (as distinguished from the everyday languages), grammar must define its own signs as far as possible. But any science (and this includes grammar), however many of its signs it defines, will be forced to end its set of definitions somewhere, with the result that the signs entering into its basically presupposed definition will not themselves be defined. Thus in every science there will remain some indefinables, or basic concepts—terms that are not defined within the scientific language itself but that can be defined only by the introduction of another language, which will be a metalanguage with respect to the language involved. So also in grammar there will remain certain basic concepts, certain undefined terms that can be defined only by the introduction of a second-degree metalanguage.

Since all the defined terms of any science must necessarily be defined by means of other terms taken from the same language, the defined terms will be fixed by their mutual relationship and can never be fixed (or even partially fixed) by their relationship to any other objects than terms within the same language. In making use of glosses from an everyday language, grammar will have the advantage over other sciences that, when it is applied to the everyday language that it itself is using, it will be able to define all the terms it has taken from the everyday language. But, as we have seen, it can define them only by their relationship to other terms within the same language, not (either in whole or in part) by their relationship to objects that are not themselves terms within the same language. Thus, the terms of grammar cannot be fixed by any things in some reality outside grammar to which they might refer or of which they are made (e.g. the electromagnetic vibrations caused by ink-marks on paper, or the sound waves caused by movements in the throat and mouth). Those, on the other hand, can be arrived at in meta-grammar, where we analyze the terms of grammar and find that the things to which they refer are the physical phenomena or other phenomena that furnish the expression and content of the object language (the everyday language) and that the things they are made of are the same as the things that the terms of other languages (e.g. the everyday language) are made of. In other words, grammar, like any other language, must be divided into a content plane and an expression plane. What constitutes the content in grammar, the content plane of grammar, is the expression and content of the everyday language. In order to treat within its content plane the expression elements and the content elements of the everyday language, grammar is obliged to introduce terms for them. It may, for example, call one expression element *p*, another *m*, and so on; and it may call one content element 'he', another 'she', another, perhaps, 'sheep', and so on. But all these terms introduced by grammar for the elements of the everyday language will remain undefined basic concepts, to be defined only in meta-grammar through an analysis of the content plane of grammar. Thus phonetics, the science of the sounds of language, and semantics, the science of the meanings of language, belong in meta-grammar. Between meta-grammar and grammar (as between any metalanguage and its object language) there is a relation of unilateral presupposition: the metalanguage presupposes the object language, and meta-grammar thus presupposes grammar. Formulated in other terms: sounds and meanings presuppose elements of expression and content; the representation presupposes what is represented.

But there is also another way in which we find languages of different degrees. If we make a grammatical analysis of a given text, provided the text is long enough (e.g. Danish literature supplemented by a large collection of recordings of spoken Danish), we shall find that within the whole text there can appear

—or by extension of the text there can be produced—fragments (either textual components of large size, or individual words, or individual elements, or individual variants) which can be translated within the text into other fragments. One fragment, perhaps, is in Jutland dialect, another in Zealand dialect; and it turns out to be possible to translate the Jutlandic fragment into Zealandic, and the Zealandic into Jutlandic. Or one fragment is written language and another spoken language, and they too can be mutually translated. Or one fragment is everyday speech, another lecture style; one fragment is prose, another poetry— in all cases, mutual translation is possible. If we had a text including different national languages, like English and Danish, we should be faced with the same situation. And the moment we have a text recorded by two different persons, we again have the same possibility of translation. Every linguistic physiognomy ("voice," "handwriting") has its own distinctive stamp, in the linguistic usage at any rate, and a text can be translated from one physiognomy to another. If I have a number of students read aloud, or relate, or write down the same story, I obtain a number of translations of one and the same text into different physiognomies.

Each time we find such a translatability between two fragments of a text, we must take account of it. Whenever we encounter different national languages, local dialects, jargons, idioms, codes, styles, or physiognomies, we must analyze separately the text that each of them has yielded, because they may reveal differences in linguistic structure. Thus, in grammar, we have to provide ourselves with a system of labeling, so that one group of texts can be marked "English" and another "Danish," or one "prose" and another "poetry," or one "John Smith" and another "James Brown," and so on—divisions which obviously cross one another in many ways. But the labels themselves— "English," "Danish," "prose," "poetry," etc.—cannot be further treated within the language of our grammar.

For the remarkable thing is that these designations stand for notions that are generally of sacral character, involving the use of a given linguistic usage or of a given linguistic structure as expression for a content consisting of certain elements that lie outside the language. Thus the Danish language is expression for a content that is the Danish nation, the family, and the home; and in the same way, different styles are expressions, or symbols, for contents consisting of certain elements that lie outside the styles. So we are again dealing with an expression and a content—with a language—but this time with a language whose expression plane is itself a language, with its own content and expression. Thus we must add to our grammar a new grammar, which treats all these "labels" (or connotators, as we shall call them) as content for a given language as expression (and we shall call this content-expression function a connotation). So here again we have to do with grammars of various degrees, but in a different sense from before. And it may be appropriate to continue along this line: in a third-degree grammar we might show what geographical, historical, social, and psychological elements compose the content of the name of a language—"Danish," for example—considered as expression for such content. Everything from national down to personal characteristic finds a natural place within the sphere of linguistics.

Linguistic genetics and linguistic typology are, of course, no different languages from grammar; they are merely extensions of its domain. Each, as we have seen, treats certain functions between the états de langue. Using the terms we have introduced above, we can summarize by saying that linguistic genetics supplies a parent language, and linguistic typology supplies a type, behind the individual languages. There is a correlation of unilateral presupposition between the individual languages and the parent language: the individual languages presuppose the parent language, but not vice versa. And the function between individual languages and parent language is a correlation, not a relation: they are not present together, but alternate. Between the individual languages and the linguistic type there is a rela-

tion of unilateral presupposition: the individual languages presuppose the linguistic type, but not vice versa. And the function
between individual language and linguistic type is a relation,
not a correlation: individual language and linguistic type are
present together; if we are given an individual language, then
in it, *eo ipso*, we are given its type. At this point we have finally
reached a *formal definition* of the two kinds of linguistic relationship: genetic relationship rests on a continuation, i.e. a correlation of unilateral presupposition between languages; typological
relationship rests on a type-realization, i.e. a relation of unilateral presupposition between languages.

# Index

'78